BEYOND BLOOD

BEYOND BLOOD

HOW BEING A FOSTER BROTHER SHATTERED MY WORLD AND REBUILT IT

MICHELLE SNYDER WITH BEN SNYDER JR.

This book is dedicated to Ben Snyder Sr., who embodies servant leadership and who knows the chapters we left unsaid. With heartfelt gratitude and love, we thank you for your support and belief in us!

Ballast Books, LLC
www.ballastbooks.com

ISBN: 978-1-962202-89-3

Printed in Hong Kong

Published by Ballast Books
www.ballastbooks.com

For more information, bulk orders, appearances, or speaking requests, please email: info@ballastbooks.com

AUTHOR'S NOTE

The author values privacy and has taken measures to protect the identities of individuals mentioned in this book. As a result, certain names and characteristics have been changed, and some events and conversations may have been condensed or reconstructed. Furthermore, certain characters might be composites based on multiple people's stories.

CONTENTS

PREFACE

WHILE WE WERE on a road trip together, I asked my son Ben (not to be confused with my husband Ben) whether he felt it had hurt him long term to be raised in a home with a revolving door of foster children. His response to me felt profound; it is undoubtedly life-changing to be a child looking into the eyes of another child who has just lost everything—and learning to be a brother to them. Sharing Ben's voice through *Beyond Blood* is intended to encourage other average families like ours. It is scary to make a radical change that places a stranger's needs before one's own family. However, our deeply personal experience led to the discovery of boundless growth and love that came from stepping out into the unknown. Other families can experience that too.

Prior to becoming a licensed foster care parent, I worked as a mental health counselor for the same population of children that we eventually brought into our home. While working on my master's degree, I provided overnight care to foster children in my apartment; I lived alone and was working and going to school as well. So, after my children were born and my husband, Ben Sr., and I began seriously discussing fostering as a family, our eyes were wide open about what to expect.

In fact, Ben Sr. was understandably wary. The conversations about fostering children had started casually several years earlier, and the whole concept was foreign to him. We talked through concerns, left and returned to the discussion many times, and even started classes to take in foster children on a few occasions before dropping out due to a mixture of fear and apathy he struggled with. I did not push him, but I did keep the conversation going.

Several years after those discussions started, we would have to place a new guideline in our home. Ben Sr. would not be the first to answer the phone for DCF when at all possible. Inevitably, he wanted to bring home every child that he heard about, regardless of available beds or seats in our cars, regardless of medical needs or the number of siblings the child would come with, and regardless of his wife's sanity. Once he forged ahead despite his paralyzing fears and concerns, Ben Sr.'s heart and mind irrevocably transformed. We were *all* the better for it.

The goal of this book is to disrupt the idea that a person should not foster or adopt because of the impact it may have on their home or family. My son Ben's story reveals the opposite—having his life turned upside-down to help the hidden children struggling in his community shaped his life in important ways.

As this story will tell, Ben's childhood was molded through kids with shocking lives arriving at his home at all hours of the night and disappearing just as abruptly. With time, he released his grip on all he believed he knew and began to see fragments of himself in the children he lived with. The toys and freedoms he sought to make him happy would no longer hold the same significance. Dental visits, family dinner nights, school days, and healthy food transitioned from impositions into gifts he was privileged to know.

Ben's young heart expanded with each child who entered our home, and he discovered a sense of resilience within himself that he would not have otherwise known existed. He learned that true strength often has nothing to do with our size. As the years went by, Ben's understanding of love deepened, and his capacity for compassion swelled through the pain we invited into our family. Every child who entered his life left an indelible mark on his soul, and as he stands on the threshold of adulthood, Ben shares his transformation and the lessons he has learned.

There is safety in stepping out, in no longer having the luxury to focus on the superficial, in setting aside personal desires to accomplish something larger. The brave children who did not have a choice but to lay their heads in a stranger's home gave Ben far more than he could ever have given them. May their voices be heard through these pages and encourage us to move beyond our comfortable fence lines.

CHAPTER ONE

IT HAD OFFICIALLY been authorized. The place I called home was now a licensed foster care residence thanks to my parents, who ignored all advice imploring them not to do it. Relatives and friends alike did not want us biological kids to become collateral damage in my parents' crazy do-gooder experiment—or at least that's more or less what my sister and I gathered from the muttered conversations we overheard.

On the one hand, I felt proud of my parents' courage, but on the other, I did not want to share my home with strangers. Mom said I had a choice, but even back then, at five years old, I felt sure there was a correct answer. So, I gave them an enthusiastic, "Yes, I want to be a foster brother!" complete with a thumbs-up and toothy smile.

My sister Annabelle, three years younger than me and tough as nails since day one, looked on while she played with a pile of blocks. She copied my confident smile and nodded her head. I knew she understood even less about what was going on than I did, but she seemed to take everything with a grain of salt. The smile was the same one Annabelle had when Mom handed her a fruit popsicle after dinner or when she showed off her bloody knee after an epic Power Wheels crash. I was glad she was there though and silently hoped that if kids really did come stay with us, they would be more interested in her toys than mine.

Later, my parents sat me down for a serious conversation. My mother paused, her voice wavering as she spoke. "Son, this will hurt; it won't be easy. Despite that, we must try to love our neighbors as ourselves. We will give them a family, and once we bring them in, you will be their brother always—no matter what."

I stared at Mom's watery eyes and nodded. She seemed aware of realities I would not understand until much later. My parents were choosing to allow suffering into my life—suffering that I wouldn't have to go through if I weren't a biological child in a foster family. Yes, I faced many hardships in this role I found myself filling. As it turned out, I would never be the same again—nor would I want to.

Not long after our talk, my parents carefully placed a newly typed list titled "Boundaries" on top of the stack of forms the Department of Children and Families (DCF) had provided. It was a painstakingly detailed document of restrictions: no infants, no teenagers, no youth with a history of violence or acting out sexually, no medically needy kids, only one child at a time. The list outlining our needs and expectations for fostering went on for pages. I could not help but feel anxious as my parents handed it all over to the social worker for processing.

But I barely had time to worry before our phone started ringing; on the other end of the line, frightened children sat next to workers waiting for a "yes." The boundaries document, which had been meticulously thought out to protect our family, ultimately proved to be a clear waste of ink. DCF contacted us about any child—or children—in need of immediate support, regardless of whether they fit the boundaries we tried to establish. The list turned out to look more like a blueprint for the children who would become brothers and sisters to me. We quickly, and unexpectedly, fell in love with them all.

The first call that came in was abrupt, and the sound of screaming pierced through the speakerphone when Mom answered. It hurt my ears, and I wished she would turn it down. Instead, Mom stood pale-faced, staring at her phone like she had not just signed up for this. As the person on the other end of the line spoke, the hum of car engines and tires rolling over asphalt could be heard in the background. The worker explained that she was sitting on the side of the highway. Baby Ray's parents had been arrested after a drug-infused brawl, and the newborn was dirty and hungry. She stated that although he was two months old, baby Ray had just been discharged from the hospital the day before due to hospital standards requiring him to weigh at least four pounds before he could go home.

My mind swirled; I did not understand how a baby who had just entered this world and who had been home with his parents for only one day could be in this bad of shape. My mom hesitantly reminded the worker that we had not signed up to take in infants, and the worker's voice faltered when she replied. "I know—I just thought I'd try."

There was stillness as Mom stared at the phone, listening to highway racket and baby wails on the other end of the line. "I'll call you back," Mom finally mumbled before hanging up.

She walked past me into Annabelle's bedroom, where Dad was rocking her to sleep. He glanced up at Mom, and they locked eyes. They had been married for a long time, so when he furrowed his brow and tilted his head slightly, Mom understood he was asking her a question. "DCF just called, honey. There's a baby."

Now Annabelle's eyes were open. She was no longer drifting off but still oblivious to the fact that our lives were about to transform.

"Okay," Dad said, but it was a question.

"The baby is two months old—four pounds." Mom continued.

My dad looked perplexed and sharpened his tone slightly, provoking Annabelle, still relaxing in his lap in the rocking chair, to jump a bit. "I thought we agreed to no infants," he said.

"Yes," Mom replied quietly, "and I will tell them no. I just wanted to let you know this baby and employee are on the highway with nowhere to go. The baby is in bad shape. The boy's parents just got arrested, and the other foster homes are full."

My dad sat mute, his gaze turned down to the carpet, his face red. After what seemed like a long while, the side of his fist came down hard onto the arm of the rocking chair, startling Annabelle and causing her pacifier to slip from her mouth into his lap. Dad handed it back to her as he quietly but firmly said, "Tell her we will take the baby."

Mom nodded and pivoted slowly to leave. It was then that she noticed me for the first time. "Oh, honey, I need you to be a big boy and put yourself down to bed tonight. Mommy is a little busy." I took it as a suggestion to stay out of her way.

Mom called the worker back, and when she discovered the baby would be coming with nothing, she dashed to Walmart to buy baby formula, bottles, diapers, wipes, a tiny blanket, a car seat and stroller, and some clothes. The articles of clothing were so small they looked like they could only be for a tiny doll.

An hour later, Annabelle had fallen asleep, and my mom had dumped all her purchases in the entryway with Dad looking on nervously. I watched through the railing as a giant chocolate woman huffed slowly into the house carrying a car seat. A tiny creature lay inside wearing only a diaper. He was no longer moving or making noise. I was scared but, at the same time, felt a strong pull toward him. The worker casually mentioned to my parents that this baby would end up going up for adoption, so we should be ready. *Adoption?* My parents looked at each other with wide eyes but said nothing.

After she left, and my dad was feeding Ray while Mom stood by, ready to assist, I headed down to them. My parents were surprised to see me, as if I had not lived here for five years and come down every night after bedtime. Nonetheless, through a heavy smile, Mom asked if I wanted to help. With gentle movements, I held Ray, fed him, and touched his baby skin, feeling his soft head, fingers, and toes. He was so tiny and fragile, and his eyes were full of innocence even though he had been through so much already. The fears my parents and I had melted away as we bathed him and held him.

A little while later, I went to bed and fell asleep quickly this time, although I did sneak into baby Ray's room once to check on him when

I woke up to use the bathroom. He was as tired as I was and did not stir as I left.

I was exhausted at school the following day and a little jealous of Ray, who had been sleeping peacefully when I left. I felt excited though. A new baby brother, and I had heard the worker say we would adopt him! I told my teachers and friends, and although they were excited with me, I could not help but get in trouble several times for talking out of turn and interrupting. I did not care—this was too important to stay quiet about!

I raced home after school and then burst into the house. Mom greeted me with a big hug, picking me right up off my feet, but there was only one thing on my mind. "I want to feed Ray again!" I said excitedly, and Mom paused tentatively, giving me a long squeeze as she held me.

My sister was eating a snack at the kitchen island nearby and did not turn around immediately. I wondered if she had gotten to play with Ray while I was gone; I wanted a turn too. Annabelle finally looked over at me and stretched her hand out, offering me one of her strawberries, but she didn't say anything either.

"Oh, sweetie," Mom replied in a gentle tone as she set me back down to stand on the floor. "Ray's gone. He was returned to his parents by a judge."

Tears sprang to my eyes, and I ran to the bedroom and looked in at the empty Pack 'n Play. Mom came up behind me and sat down in the rocking chair. I could tell she wanted to be a comforting presence as I processed this unexpected news.

Apparently, Ray's dad had gotten out of jail in the morning, and since he was friends with a local judge, he had received small-town justice—drug possession and battery charges dropped and baby Ray back in their apartment.

"I love you," Mom murmured, wrapping me in a hug. Unsure of what else to say, she followed that up with, "We're having spaghetti tonight for dinner."

Annabelle had climbed down from her stool and walked into the room where we were standing. She hugged me too and said, "I love you, Bunny," using her nickname for me. I stood still, wiping back a few tears that had traveled down my face.

"Okay," I replied mechanically. Then, I let Mom hold me for a while longer as my mind swirled, trying to make sense of everything that had happened. Little did I know this was just the first of many sudden goodbyes to new brothers and sisters I'd gain through our family's experience with the foster care system.

CHAPTER TWO

DCF STARTED CALLING every day, and when Mom did not answer, they got ahold of Dad. A lot of the calls were for older teenagers, large sibling groups, and kids with significant medical needs that we had no idea how to care for. My parents still discussed and considered each one, though, from my perspective, reading and following their boundaries list would have saved them a lot of heated discussions and tears that inevitably came up due to these calls. Although my parents seemed to know intellectually that some of the kids that DCF called us about really weren't the right fit, they still tortured themselves over saying no. Mom and Dad felt guilty saying no to anyone, and I could see they were a lot quieter and distracted after we would turn down a placement.

On the flip side, when we got to say yes, we all had more energy and focus, with everyone ready to set down what they were doing and prepare to help this little one together. Even Annabelle took her favorite stuffed animal and put it in the new girl's bed to comfort her before we left to bring her home.

We picked Sophie up from the Olive Garden on a Sunday afternoon. When we drove into the parking lot, we spotted a lady who, as we'd come to find out, did not speak English standing outside a beat-up white Honda Civic holding her. Mom got out and approached

Sophie, who looked like she had been through a lot. Her dress was worn and faded, and it looked like she had outgrown it a while back. She was clutching a raggedy stuffed cloth, so worn out I couldn't make out what it used to be—maybe a bear or dog. It was mostly threads, and she unexpectedly offered it to Mom as she reached for her. Mom gently settled the stuffed cloth back in the crook of Sophie's arm and took Sophie instead. The toddler went straight into Mom's arms without hesitation or any change of expression.

Annabelle said hi to Sophie. Then, she reached up and took her hand and smiled at her for a moment. I noted that Annabelle looked and acted much older than Sophie, although they were only a few months apart.

Dad pushed my booster seat back to the third row so Sophie could be closer to Mom and Dad. Annabelle got to sit next to her in her own car seat, and she was happy to have Sophie beside her. To our surprise, Sophie did not cry when we buckled her into her car seat or later that night when we put her to bed in the Pack 'n Play (one of the slats had broken on the old crib, and my parents were waiting on a new one to get delivered). She didn't even cry when we took her to get her vaccines and they gave her four shots at once.

We soon realized she never cried. She also never got full and seemed to enjoy eating until she threw up, so Mom had to move my plate away from hers so she would stop stealing food from me. Annabelle was scolded a few times because she kept slipping Sophie food that she didn't want to eat at dinner. The ruse worked for a while until Dad got too suspicious about how Annabelle had suddenly started cleaning her plate at every meal. He started watching them closer, and pretty soon, Sophie had a whole section of the kitchen table to herself, not within arm's reach of us other kids, to help her avoid overeating and getting sick again.

Mom also took time to explain that Sophie had been neglected as a baby. The police had found her alone in a wrecked car in a pawn shop parking lot. To their horror, they determined she had been sitting there by herself for many hours even though she was only two.

Sophie had a heart condition we did not know about until after she moved in, so she was sick a lot. She threw up on my parents and their friends, and she frequently had a fever and caught everything going around, so my parents had to give her special attention. We played with LEGOs and painted together, and I even let her ride shotgun in my Hot Wheels car.

Then, one day, I woke up with my whole chest covered in red bumps. I tried to call out for Mom, but my throat hurt too much to speak.

My mom's response when she saw me was not reassuring. "Oh no—you have it now too?"

Sophie had contracted scarlet fever for the second time, and on this occasion, she had shared this unfortunate gift with me. I was already uncomfortable since we all had pink eye. First, Sophie got it. Then, Mom got it in both of her eyes to the extent that she could not see much of anything for a while.

Annabelle also woke up with her eyes crusted shut and didn't want anyone to touch her face, so she bumped into walls and walked around only half-sighted until Mom grabbed her. She had to hold Annabelle down and put a warm washcloth over her eyes for a while to help her see again.

Dad was the smart one; he took a pillow and some clothes and his laptop to the futon in the office, declaring he couldn't get sick since he had to work and provide for the family. He parented us by talking through the glass door separating the office and the living room, but he wouldn't come out or touch us. He never got sick. I told him to let me in before I got pink eye too, but he said I'd already been too exposed, and he couldn't risk it . . . and he was right. Not long after, my eyes started itching and turning red too. I complained loudly and often—it felt like sandpaper in my eyes.

Sophie was different though. She never complained when she was sick. She just kept looking for food. Sophie lived with us for a year, during which time we took in two more foster sisters. Then, the judge said it was time for Sophie's birth mom to take her back. Just like that, she was gone.

Dad drove her to an office and handed her over even though Sophie cried, yelled "Daddy," and held onto his clothes. He came home quiet and serious, and his mood did not lift for a few days. Mom barely got out of bed. I heated mac and cheese for Annabelle and myself, and we ate big bowls of cereal we were normally only allowed once a day. We also enjoyed some unexpected time off from school since Mom either forgot to take us or could not get up.

Mom tried to help Sophie's birth mom. They talked on the phone, and she told Mom that Sophie had tried to run away from her in Walmart the day before. When she'd seen someone who looked like my dad, Sophie had started screaming "Daddy!" and chasing after him through the store.

As it turned out, we did not help Sophie's mom much at all. She overdosed on drugs and died in their trailer after her daughter was home for a total of one week, leaving Sophie crawling around again with no one to watch out for her. We learned this from a neighbor of hers, the one who found them. Although Mom tried, we never found out what happened to Sophie after that or heard from her again. A DCF worker had come and gone from their trailer with her after the neighbor called the police, and from there, Sophie was dropped off in another county at an undisclosed home. According to Mom, the worker had seen no record of Sophie living with us before when they placed her in another town.

Sophie had been my sister for half her life, and my mom had told everyone who would listen we were always here if needed, so how could she suddenly disappear forever? I would go to sleep asking myself that question, wondering what was the point of taking in kids when everything seemed to end so painfully, when the brothers and sisters that shared our home with us just ended up in the same situations or worse after they left. Though I did not get an answer right away, I would eventually get used to these things, and as I grew, I came to understand.

CHAPTER THREE

A WEEK LATER, I was told I would have a new foster brother—a gypsy, according to my dad. I was eager to meet this gypsy brother who was my age and hoped he liked jumping on the trampoline too.

He arrived with no shoes or shirt. I instantly noted that he smelled weird and appeared to be very hungry. He had a big, purple, swollen bruise under his right eye, and he did not talk and did not smile, which I completely understood. I knew that he was likely scared and tired. When I asked him what happened to his face, Mom scolded me immediately, saying it was not socially appropriate. I tried to argue with her about it being the most relevant thing to say when someone you are caring for is injured, but she kept shushing me. Finally, I gave up.

Mom cooked him some food and got him situated with a plate. Fenix ate fast, as if someone might take the food from him before he could get his fill. I sat beside him and tried to chat with him, but he paid me little attention.

When Fenix took a sip of his drink, he suddenly pulled his arm back and threw his water glass. It grazed the side of my head and smashed into the fridge behind me. Everyone in the room jumped except Fenix, who kept eating. He still had not spoken.

Mom chuckled nervously. "Guess he's not a fan of water." Without any further commentary, she cleaned up the mess.

Fenix kept eating as though nothing had happened. After a moment, I retrieved a nearby baseball and handed it to him, asking if he wanted to play catch after he ate. I always tried to find ways to help the new kids relax and get out of their shells when they arrived. Playing with my new siblings was a way to connect with them without having to talk about hard stuff up front. Fenix did not look at me but kept eating, and Mom gave me a reassuring smile. I looked back at Fenix in time to see him pull his arm back and throw the ball directly at my head with an angry scream. Since I was sitting so close to him, the ball slammed into my face, and I felt a sharp pain followed instantly by a warm sensation. Everyone jumped up at once.

"That wasn't an accident," Dad said urgently to Mom, who was already pushing me back from Fenix and putting a towel over my bloody face.

She leaned down to eye level with Fenix and said, "No hitting, please." Fenix responded by quickly slapping Mom in the face, all while munching on his chicken nuggets.

Annabelle, the tough one in the group, couldn't take anymore. She jumped down and screamed as she ran to Fenix with both arms above her head and her hands balled into fists. Dad dropped the bloody towel he held over my face and grabbed Annabelle just in time, lifting her off her feet as she swung at the air. Mom quickly declared that Fenix needed to go to time out, and she walked him to his room to talk to him. "We do not hit here. This is a safe place for everyone. I will be back in five minutes, and we can try again. I'm sorry you're sad, and I hope we can help you feel better." She leaned in to hug him; he jumped back. She gave an understanding nod and walked out.

It was only about thirty seconds later that we heard a piercing scream. We rushed to Fenix's room to see he had stripped off all his clothes. He was naked and running around the room, ripping the TV off its mount, knocking over his bed, and kicking the walls. He was alarmingly strong. He screamed again—an ear-piercing noise that seemed to echo through the whole house.

After a moment of shock, Mom got low on the ground, almost sitting, and moved toward Fenix. "You're okay, buddy," she soothed. "Can I help you put your clothes on?"

Fenix ran to Mom, leaping on her and punching, kicking, scratching. Mom yelled at Dad to get the other kids away, repeating "STOP" over and over while trying to get him off her. Finally, he turned his frustrations back to the wall, and Mom retreated from the room again.

After cleaning up the scratches and blood on her face and mine, Mom sat me down. I could tell she was trying not to cry. She smiled weakly as she spoke. "Thank you for trying to be a good friend to Fenix; he is scared and confused now. I want to explain something to you, honey. Fenix has lived in a car his whole life, just driving around to unusual places that were not always safe, and his parents hurt each other when they feel angry. They hurt each other in front of him in the car, and that is why he is staying with us. Sometimes, they hurt him too. Fenix does not know that it is not normal to hit; he is replaying what he learned from his family. That being said, you cannot play with Fenix alone until we can help him feel more stable here. Everything will be okay."

She hugged me for a long time, and I could feel she was fighting back tears. My stomach hurt, my head hurt, my heart hurt. Silently acknowledging my pain, she changed the bandage on my forehead before encouraging me to go to bed.

It was Dad's turn to help Fenix settle in. Mom asked him to try to give Fenix a bath and tuck him into bed. However, my foster brother was asleep naked on the floor when Dad entered the room. Dad just moved him into the bed, covered him up, and let him sleep, saying sleep was important and we would try again in the morning.

To everyone's disappointment, the morning was no better, as Fenix picked up his breakfast and threw it against the wall. Mom tried desperately to get Fenix to talk. However, she and Dad said they weren't sure whether he spoke English, and when they called and asked the worker who had dropped him off, she had no idea either. Although she had picked Fenix up from the police the night before, they hadn't spoken on the ride to our house. She was not sure what language the parents spoke, but she assured us she would investigate it.

The next few days went much the same. Fenix, it turned out, spoke only a language of violence as far as we could figure out, and we did not know how to help him. A new rule was in place at our house: no kids could go near Fenix, even to play.

Every day, Fenix acted violently with no provocation or warning, and the attacks were so fast it was hard to know what was happening until it was over. Every night, my parents gently tried to comfort him, sit on the floor, and engage him in games or books, showing they were safe. Yet, every night, Fenix would strip naked, screaming and damaging things around him. Then, when he would get tired and pass out, Mom or Dad would move him into his bed. In the morning, Fenix was always asleep on the floor once again.

Eventually, my parents stopped moving him into bed. They explained that Fenix had never slept in a bed. It felt uncomfortable to him, so we needed to let him sleep on the floor if that helped him. Mom put a foam mat, blanket, and pillow on the floor, but Fenix rejected even this, preferring some chaotic mess where he was half lying against a hard wall and half sitting up.

I watched him sleep curled up in a ball against the wall one morning, and my heart just ached for him and all he had gone through. I thought about how uncomfortable falling asleep in the car was on the way home from school, how my neck would hurt when I got out; I could not imagine sleeping like that my whole life.

Then, I thought about times I had complained about getting in my big, soft bed at night. Now, I was ashamed of how ungrateful I had been. I had resented being made to eat fresh meals my parents provided and even complained about having to pick up my toys at the end of the day. Whenever a new season approached, I was irritated by Mom's shopping trips; I knew she would come home with a bag of clothes and expect me to try everything on. Then, she would inspect each item to make sure they fit. I would complain and rush her, wanting to get back to my cartoons or my toys.

My parents had always told me not to be ungrateful, had always said we were extremely fortunate. It never sank in until I was forced to learn firsthand what they meant. I was taught by victimized children who were desperate for the things I took for granted. I knew at that moment I could have been Fenix, and he could have been me. I could have been born into a different family. Guilt settled deep in my gut, although I tried to push it away. These kids were my brothers and sisters now, but they had always been my neighbors. Before we became a foster family, I'd never seen them, hadn't even known they existed, but that did not dull the truth.

Mom could not put Fenix in daycare, leave him with babysitters, or get a break at all due to his behavior. My parents tried to take him to their adult Sunday school class, but he just hit them and hurled their keys, phones, or any belongings he could sneak a hand onto at the back of other people's heads. After a few weeks of this, my parents made a call. Fenix needed more help than we could give him, and shortly after that, we received the name of another foster family with whom we were supposed to drop him off.

Three days later, Dad packed up the clothes and toys we had bought Fenix, and Mom left to take him to his new home. A few hours later, Mom returned looking very distressed, saying the family he was moved to were brand-new foster parents with small children, and they did not have the details about Fenix's situation yet when Mom had arrived.

I felt sad and anxious for the new foster family and for Fenix as well. I wondered what his life would be like, and although I felt like a weight had been lifted off my shoulders, I also felt guilty admitting even to myself that I was glad he was gone. I was mad at him, and I was confused. I wanted to blame him for the problems he'd caused, but I was starting to understand he was a victim too, and his behavior was not really his fault.

After Fenix left, I often thought about him and wished things could have been different—that we could have found a way to help Fenix or make him happy. But that was not the way this story had played out. Our home felt peaceful again on the surface without his outbursts and violent behavior, but my heart was growing more confused by the day.

I spent the next several days digging a backyard swimming pool with Annabelle, trying to forget about everything we had just been through. We had been obsessed with the idea of having our own pool for a while; Florida was perpetually hot, and we were always looking for a way to cool off. My parents were much less enthusiastic about my new focus, though, to their credit, they let us have our fun.

After several days of digging up all our grass outside the back door, we were ready. I dragged the hose out to the mud pit and turned it on. With gleeful anticipation, Annabelle and I watched eagerly as our pool filled up. It may not have been as glamorous as an actual swimming pool, but it was ours, and we were beyond excited. It turned out even better than we had expected, and we jumped straight into our mud bath and played for hours. We splashed each other and horsed around until we were completely covered from head to toe in muddy water.

My parents watched with amusement and even applauded our efforts, although Dad mumbled under his breath about having to resod the yard. Before he could say anything more, Mom shot him a look that promptly silenced him.

Dad did come home a few days later with his truck filled with sod pallets and a horse trough. He opened the gate to our backyard and drove his truck through until he was at the back of our four-acre property. We ran to see what he was up to. Dad climbed out of the truck and opened the tailgate, yanking the horse trough out and dropping it unceremoniously onto the ground.

"What is this for, Dad? Are we getting a horse?" I asked.

"Nope," Dad replied with a smile. "It's a pool for you. Enjoy!" He hopped back into the truck and drove back toward the house, leaving my sister and I standing there in disbelief.

After looking at each other with wide eyes for a second, we eagerly bounded into the empty horse trough, excited to check out our new pool. We yelled for Dad to bring us water, and eventually, he connected some hoses to fill the trough. While the water level steadily rose, we dashed into the house and ransacked our beach bag. Moments later, Annabelle and I darted back outside carrying dive sticks, floaties, water balls, and everything we could think of to throw in the horse trough.

It was cold and refreshing when we jumped in, and we loved it. It took Dad a couple of days to fill up our old pool with new sod, so we ran back and forth between our two pools, laughing and splashing around. Even our weekend foster placements that we unexpectedly ended up with loved it and joined in the excitement.

Eventually, however, our fun ended. Dad covered up our mud pool with new sod, and one day, the horse trough turned our skin a light shade of green. Even though Dad offered to refill it with clean water and a chlorine tab, Mom declined his offer for us. But I'll never forget those days that helped divert my mind from the confused hurt I felt after Fenix left our home.

CHAPTER FOUR

THE BRUISES AND lacerations on me, my mom, and my dad had not totally healed, and the wall repairs in Fenix's old room had not yet been completed, when I came down for breakfast one Saturday not long after the horse trough pool had been turned upside down and abandoned. On the couch watching cartoons was a kid I had never seen before. He was little with deep brown skin, a mohawk-shaped afro, and a diamond stud in his left ear. I was too tired to ask questions, and apparently, so was he. After the briefest eye contact with each other, he shifted his gaze back to the TV, and I walked past him and poured myself a bowl of cereal.

My sister was already at the table eating, and she never mentioned him either. It was as though he had always been with us, and it was an average Saturday. I guess, in a way, it *was* an average Saturday for us, although after Fenix's time with us, I was a bit more wary.

I did not see Dad that morning, and Mom slept in her room next to the living room with the door open. It was obvious that she'd had a late night with DCF again. After Mom finally woke up and poured herself a cup of coffee, she called me over and explained what had happened.

Demarious's parents were separated, and they were fighting so badly over him—even stealing him from each other—that a judge put him in state custody. The fighting had turned physical, and Demarious had been struck and injured during a violent argument between his parents.

After going over the basics with me, Mom explained, "He has severe asthma, and he was dropped here with no inhaler or paperwork. We need to keep him super calm. Don't upset him or get him moving around too much until I can get an inhaler or some more information on him and can get him to a doctor."

Demarious, it turned out, was seven years old but extremely small for his age. Regardless of his size, he was strong, remarkably athletic, and obsessed with sports balls. He liked having me around, so we threw the football and baseball and shot baskets a lot. Mom was always trying to get us to slow down and play calmly—with little success. I was happy to have a brother, even if he was more athletic than me. He was in the car on the days when Mom picked me up from school, and we were always happy to see each other and resume our games.

We fought sometimes too. Mom said we were both stubborn and rough with each other, and we needed to learn to keep our hands to ourselves. Our bickering never lasted long though; we would get back to playing quickly. We enjoyed spending time together too much to stay mad for long.

One Saturday, Mom announced that it would be the perfect day for Demarious to learn to ride a bike and that Dad was a great teacher. Dad glanced up from his hunting magazine and shot Mom a look. But she tilted her head, smiled brightly, and offered to videotape. So Dad put on his tennis shoes and advised Demarious to do the same. Demarious did not necessarily want to learn to ride a bike, but Mom said it was a valuable skill, and since he was already seven, it was time.

We walked to the front porch as a group, and I jumped on my bike and rode in circles to demonstrate. My dad grabbed Annabelle's little pink bike with training wheels and streamers, complete with a basket adorned with a unicorn, and told Demarious to get on. But instead of jumping on, he pointed accusingly at the bike.

"Why you tryin' to put me on this pink piece of shit?! I ain't gonna be seen on no unicorn bike!"

Dad tried weakly to defend the bike, but before he could say much, I interjected. "Hey, I bet if you ride the bike, then Dad and Mom will give you ice cream as a reward." I knew he loved ice cream and almost never got it before coming to our house. He only sparingly got it now since my parents tended to prepare healthier options for us.

With that, Demarious's face changed, and he looked up at Dad questioningly. "Yes," Dad agreed, glancing at Mom. "I'll give you ice cream if you ride the bike."

So, Demarious happily climbed on the pink piece-of-shit unicorn bike and tried to take off—before promptly falling straight over into a bush, where he lay cursing. Dad picked him up, and for the next hour, he ran up and down the driveway with Demarious pretending to pedal and steer. Throughout the entire experience, Dad was halfway carrying the bike and Demarious, and it wasn't long before he declared it was ice cream time. I was quite sure what had happened outside would not have qualified as actually riding a bike, but Dad was done, and Mom did not want to get cursed out by a seven-year-old anymore that day, so we prepared bowls of ice cream and called it a job well done.

Dad practiced with Demarious a few more times in the weeks after that, and one day, Demarious approached me saying it was time to "ride or die." I looked at him like he was crazy but followed him as he walked outside. He grabbed the streamer handlers and walked the unicorn bike down our driveway and into the road, all the way to the hill on the next street over. He jumped on, and I handed him the bike's matching pink helmet to cover his mohawk afro, wishing I had some way to record this moment and wondering how bad his injuries would be this time. Based on the determined gleam in his eye, I knew I was not talking him out of this scheme, and I was curious to see what happened anyway.

"Give me a push," he instructed me steadily. I did not hesitate in case he might change his mind. When I shoved him down the hill, he immediately screamed at me, "Motherfucker, whyyyyyy?" But it was too late for a chat. He was rapidly traveling down the hill, and he screamed as the bike shook wildly back and forth. But to my great surprise, he stayed on, and eventually, the hill evened out. No longer screaming, he put his feet down and scraped his shoes next to him to stop. "Woo-hoo!" he crowed triumphantly.

"You did it!" I cheered as I ran to him. We laughed and hugged and walked the bike back up the hill several times so he could jump back on and fly down again, screaming things like "Ride or die, bitches!" coupled with happy shrieks as he barely stayed up.

We went home an hour later and rode back and forth on our big driveway together, showing our parents his new skill. Dad was so proud of him that he came home from work the next day with a blue and red bike boasting a Spider-Man logo and a horn plus a glow-in-the-dark mohawk helmet. Demarious kicked Annabelle's bike, declaring it a hunk of junk one last time before jumping on his new ride. We rode every day after that without fail, getting farther and farther from home each day, now with permission from my parents.

One day after school, a DCF worker took Demarious to a meeting. She said it would be quick, so Mom got dinner ready, and we waited for Demarious to return. After a few hours, it got dark, and we ate without him.

After dinner, Mom and Dad sat on the porch, looking down the street. My brother was long overdue to get home. Mom tried calling the worker who had taken him, but it went to voicemail. Determined to get some answers, she called the DCF on-call number, but the person who answered could not find a file on Demarious. They said they would call back when they located his file, but they never did. We were worried sick by bedtime. Mom had Annabelle and me pick up Demarious's toys for him while she covered his dinner up and put it in the refrigerator. Then, we prayed as a family for him.

I went to sleep. Based on the way they looked the next morning, I do not think my parents ever slept that night.

The next day, Mom called every number she could find and eventually got a DCF transporter on the phone. "Oh, the little boy with the mohawk and diamond earring? A worker told me to drop him off at an apartment address in Kissimmee. I guess it was a relative." Before Mom could hang up, a text came through her phone. The worker from yesterday had penned this message: *Judge changed D's shelter order unexpectedly at meeting, so driver dropped him w/ a friend of dad's. Didn't want to make two trips. Sorry—forgot to tell u.*

And just like that, Demarious was gone from our lives, his clothes, toys, and Spider-Man bike as well as last night's dinner the only evidence left of my brother. My parents were in shock and could not get any more information. Meanwhile, I had so many emotions jumbled together that I did not know how I felt. I knew the goal was for him to be with his biological parents, but a random friend? Mom explained it was seen as preferable for a child not to formally be in DCF custody if possible, and this was a way to achieve that goal. Even though the person he went to was a stranger to Demarious and he had bonded with our family while we waited for his parents to heal their lives and be ready to take him home, the decision had been made.

I was angry at God and at the world. Why did all these hard things keep happening to kids around me? Why hadn't I known about it before? Why couldn't I help them more? Why were their lives so confusing and unfair? What was the point of everything we were doing if the kids we tried to help went right back into bad situations—like giving them hope and ripping it away?

I clenched my fists, my knuckles turning white with frustration. I was six now, and already, my spirit felt crushed. It seemed like I was being awakened to a harsh reality that had been unknown to me prior to us becoming a foster care home. My eyes were opened now since I was doing life with a community of people that had been hidden before.

My parents making the decision to ignore the advice of everyone they knew and bring hurting children to our house to live had turned so many things I thought I knew upside down. I had thought I could help—thought we could make a difference. I knew I was small, though I was getting older much faster now that my house was a foster home. The mission my parents were on, fueled by compassion, made me feel a desperate need to change something in myself to survive this. I had no words for any of this at the time.

Years later, I would understand the importance of these moments. They taught me that the time we had with loved ones should not be taken for granted, reminded me to appreciate those around us while we can and to know we aren't guaranteed tomorrow.

CHAPTER FIVE

I HOPPED ON my bike and pedaled as hard as I could into the field down the street from my house. With every pump of my legs, I saw the shattered hopes and broken dreams of kids, of their families, of my family—all intertwined now. My heart weighed heavy. This journey was stealing my faith, leaving a hollow ache of confusion and unanswered prayer. Overcome with frustration, I tried to jump off my bike and fell, my face hitting the dirt. I yelled at the sky, punched the ground, and let tears come. "I need to understand!" I shouted again and again. At my age, there were no words to match what my soul needed to get out, so I cried and lay in the dirt.

I fell asleep in the field, and the next time I opened my eyes, my mom was walking up to me where I lay. I do not know how she found me. I did not move, and for a minute, it was quiet while she simply looked at me. She seemed to be trying to figure out whether she was supposed to be mad that I had disappeared or worried about what I was doing. Her face softened, and then she came to me, sitting down beside me in the dirt and putting my head in her lap. "Are you sad about Demarious leaving?"

I did not answer her.

"Ben, the kids that come live with us are getting to see what safe adults look like. They are getting to experience hope for their future.

They are getting to lay down their burdens for a bit and be little, play, get cleaned off, learn about trust and unconditional love. They are getting to experience moments of happiness and not just survival. If they have periods in their life when they experience this, then maybe, when they grow up, they can hold onto these things and even share them with others instead of clinging to the hurt they have been given. Most kids that come to us will continue their journey with complicated and hard lives, so let's try to be a well of refreshment along the way. I think that's what you, Dad, and Annabelle and I are supposed to do."

I was quiet for a long time. In my mind, I saw the moments of peace she referred to and understood that would have to be the goal instead of expecting a straight and continuous road of peace and stability for these brothers and sisters. I understood what she was trying to say. But I did not tell her. I just poured everything out. I asked about the people who were mad at us, who thought we were trying to steal their kids—the ones who accused us of hurting the kids we took in when we were just trying to help. I asked about the friends we had lost because they did not want their families around our messy lives now. I even brought up the kids who had blamed us for not being able to go home when our whole goal was to help them get home.

"Ben," Mom murmured. "Look at Jesus's life. He died to help those who were accusing him. We are making a difference, even if it is hard to see. We must believe it; let's keep trying." We sat until the sun dipped below the horizon, casting long shadows across the field. "You are changing, and that is hard. But it is not bad. Keep moving forward and keep asking the tough questions." In a quieter voice, she added, "And please let me know where you're going next time. I was worried sick."

As I rode my bike home, I thought about whether I really was changing. I knew it was true.

I had noticed my parents changing too. They had always loved each other, and Annabelle and I often pretended to gag and complain when they showed affection in front of us, but before we started fostering, they'd also had their fair share of clashes. They weren't major fights or anything—just silly disagreements over trivial things. My parents both had an independent streak and too much confidence in their own positions. What to feed us kids, when we should go to bed, how to load the dishwasher, or whether to buy a new rug could end in debate. The squabbles were about nonconsequential topics, but the tension was real.

Dad had looked at Mom one day during a heated discussion on whether it was time to replace the microwave and asked an excellent question. "Michelle, our foster care license will come through any day now. How are we going to bring kids into this house to live if we're having all these stupid disagreements about little things? No one is going to want to be around that!"

Mom's face turned red, and she opened her mouth to respond impulsively—but stopped. She thought for a minute. Then, she replied, "I don't think the kids are able to wait for the perfect family, Ben. If kids did not go into homes where the adults had some disagreements, there would be no foster homes anyway." She sighed. "Just leave the duct tape on the microwave door then. You are right—it does not matter." With that, she turned and left the room.

What neither of them expected though was that when we entered the world of fostering, it changed them too. Maybe it was because they had to work together as a team to navigate all the challenges that came with fostering vulnerable children. Or maybe it was because they saw firsthand how much these children needed love and stability, and they did not want to waste any time arguing over petty things.

Whatever the reason, I witnessed a shift in their relationship after we began taking in foster children. They became more patient with each other, more understanding and supportive. They learned how to compromise and communicate effectively. And most importantly, they learned to lean on each other during tough times. The moments when they needed to work something out, they would go sit on our outdoor porch and talk, but even that was rarely needed now.

As we welcomed more foster children into our home, I could see my parents growing closer together. They laughed more often and shared inside jokes about our crazy adventures as a foster family. They also became better at handling conflicts with grace and compassion. And when one of them broke down, the other one held them tight. No one expected bringing more stress into our family would decrease other stress within our home, but that was the way it played out.

The house was quiet when my mom and I walked back in from our talk in the field, and I wanted to crash, too tired to eat dinner or even think anymore. Dad made me shower and drink some soup, and then I slept hard.

We had no real time to recover though. The next day, as I ate breakfast, the phone rang. The dust hadn't even settled, and there were my parents again, talking in hushed voices, Dad running his hands through his hair nervously, and Mom shaking her head. Eventually, they came into the kitchen, where I was working on a puzzle. They tried hard to act casual, which is how I knew something not casual at all was going on. I guessed the topic but not the details.

It was another foster sister. This time, she was older than me—twelve—but Dad said it would not seem like it. When I looked confused, he explained somewhat poorly that she had microencephaly, and in her brain, she was younger than me. Dad said he had Googled it to learn more. Mom listened with eyebrows raised and the tiniest smile as he explained to us that she would be smaller than normal and her brain would be younger than mine, and that was pretty much what he had gotten from the web article. Well, I was not sure how this fit into the boundaries we had all established, but I shrugged and said, "Okay."

When Sharon showed up the next day, we immediately noted that she was not small. In fact, I could tell my parents were as surprised as I was when a girl almost my dad's size lumbered out of the back seat with a huge grin on her face. "Hi—I love you!" she trilled as she bear-hugged my parents and me.

Dad always liked to tell us not to believe everything we read on the internet, and I took the opportunity to remind him of his own teachings. He glared at me, unamused.

Sharon chimed in—"I made you something!"—and she presented us with a torn sheet of paper with crayon scribbled on it. Mom really loved it and hung it on the fridge right away. "I love dogs!" Sharon said and sat on the floor to play with our dogs.

The DCF transporter had followed us in and handed over a bag of pills. "Here is Sharon's medication," she announced. My parents then found out for the first time that Sharon also had epilepsy and took medication several times a day to prevent seizures. The color drained from Mom's face as she nodded to the worker and closed the door behind her. Sharon was laughing hysterically while our dog licked her and bounced around.

Sharon was always happy and excited about everything. She was fun to be around. Together, we took the dogs for a walk, jumped on the trampoline, drew with sidewalk chalk, and helped Mom make dinner. Sharon and Annabelle did each other's makeup and played dolls and loved to watch cartoons together. Even though Sharon was a hundred pounds heavier and a few feet taller than Annabelle, they loved being sisters and made up a secret handshake to cement their friendship. My parents were laughing and smiling more frequently too; Sharon made everyone around her feel happy.

One day, not long after she arrived, Dad announced he needed to go to Costco for groceries and asked me to come along. "I want to come too! I want to help!" Sharon announced in a loud and eager voice. Dad and Mom smiled and glanced at each other. After the slightest nod from Mom, Dad declared that he would love Sharon's help.

We clambered into Dad's truck and took off. Sharon was always happy—and always loud. She *always* used her outdoor voice. When we were at the store, she pointed to every item on the shelf and asked if Dad wanted her to put it in the cart. Dad had already filled up a huge cart, and since Sharon was as big as him, and since she needed to be distracted, he asked her to push it for him.

When we got to a section marked "pharmacy," Dad stopped in his tracks, causing Sharon to run into him. He was unfazed. Turning slowly, he said, "Sharon, Mommy Michelle gave you your medicine this morning, right?"

Sharon squeezed her eyes shut tightly. When she reopened them, she happily yelled, "No medicine today!" like she was announcing we were getting ice cream later.

Dad's eyes got big and started darting around the store. He opened his phone and called Mom. When he hung up, he announced that we had everything we needed and that it was time to leave right away. I asked if Sharon was going to have a seizure in Costco since she had not taken her medicine. Dad gave me a look that told me to shut up, but I felt like I had just asked an excellent question.

Sharon became even more excited. "Oh, I might have a seizure! Oh, wow!" she announced loudly.

I could see Dad sweating as we stood in the long checkout line, waiting our turn.

"Dad, shouldn't we be getting her medicine so she doesn't die here or something?" I exclaimed loudly, pulling on his arm. I could not believe he was just standing there; I was scared. I'd heard what the worker had said.

"You are not helping—I told you to be quiet. STOP TALKING!" Dad snapped at me. There was no doubt that everyone was staring at us now.

"Oh, I might die!" Sharon said cheerfully. "Oh, wow, I might have a seizure and die!"

It was finally our turn, and Sharon insisted on lifting the fifty-pound bags of dog food and big water jugs up to the conveyer. She made it seem easy, which did not surprise me since she looked like she could pick up Dad easily too. Dad threw everything back in the cart after we paid and made us jog to the car with him. After all three of us had haphazardly launched our purchases into the back of the truck, Dad urged us to get in, and he peeled out of the parking lot.

Dad usually drives slow, but today, we got home in record time. When we pulled onto our street, he called Mom and asked her to meet us out front. She was waiting with medicine and a glass of water as Dad lurched into the driveway. Sharon was hanging out the window, yelling, "I didn't die, Mom! Daddy Ben forgot my medicine, but I didn't die—I'm still right here!" Mom smiled and congratulated Sharon and gave her the medicine before she could even get out of the truck.

Sharon was more than a sister to me; she was my friend and teacher. Sharon loved the things I loved: our family, our pets, and spending time together. Her bright smile and infectious laugh lit up our home. Despite this, she was not always well-liked. It pained me when people, including some kids that I had once called my friends, would mock her and mimic her voice. Annabelle was so much younger that she didn't seem to realize how cruel people were being to Sharon. Sharon didn't seem to understand either at times.

It was different for me though. It stoked a fire of defensiveness in me for Sharon and for other kids like her. But when I sat with those feelings, I knew in my heart there was a chance I might have casually done the same if I had not come to understand that Sharon's unique abilities gave her the gentle soul and the warmth she carried with her. I realized people who stared at her or made fun of her were missing the true beauty of my sister. I did not know how to convey this to my friends yet; despite my inner turmoil, I said nothing to defend her. Looking back, the guilt I felt at the time, and that I still feel about my inaction, stays under the surface and compels me to now speak up for others when I am able.

We knew Sharon's time with our family was ending, and when her departure date arrived, my heart was pained for me and glad for her. Dad called this goodbye bittersweet. We had a pizza party with an ice cream dessert to celebrate her transition. Sharon's biological mom had gotten a job and a place to live and was ready for her daughter now, and DCF believed she was in a good place to care for Sharon's medical needs. We were incredibly happy for them both. The transition was one of the most peaceful ones out of all the brothers and sisters that shared our home with us.

It was a gift, and I try to carry a piece of Sharon's unique spirit with me. I will always be thankful for the lessons she taught me about acceptance, compassion, and the simple joys in life, even at such an early age.

CHAPTER SIX

ON SUNDAY MORNING, we went to church as usual. We had two new kids who were just staying with us for the weekend. They had been kidnapped from Colorado by a relative and were found living in a car near us. A DCF worker was flying in from Colorado to escort them back home to their parents. They were excited to stay with us for the weekend and to head back to Colorado. Despite the situation, they felt they were on a grand adventure overall. I did not totally understand this nonchalance, but I was happy that they were happy. So, we tried to make it a fun weekend, watching movies and popping popcorn.

Then, off we went to church. We visited a few different ones, and they all felt pretty similar to me. It always made me self-conscious—our family looked different from everyone else's, and we got lots of stares and questions about my brothers and sisters. Dad explained people meant well, and I knew they did. Their stares came with curious smiles, and we always got bags of their kids' old clothes as donations to help. We tried our best to look nice, but we were never going to blend in going out in public. Kids with different skin colors than us, injuries, special needs, a bent toward tantrums and bad language—there was just no way we were going to fly under the radar. Church went as expected, and Dad offered to take us out to eat afterward, but Mom said she needed a nap.

For a while, Mom had been struggling to get out of bed, and she wasn't eating much. I also noticed she would not put makeup on like she does when she is happy. She wouldn't even do dishes or laundry. I had gotten used to it since this was how she always reacted when kids left. But on this day, Dad announced we needed more support. Mom's heart seemed too tired to question it. So late that afternoon, he loaded us back up into the car and headed out. Then, that evening, we went to church again but this time in a different building. He had been encouraged by a friend to check out a congregation already involved in the work our family was doing. Dad was struggling to keep us all afloat, and so he wanted to give it a shot.

When we walked in, we saw kids like us everywhere, running around and playing tag while parents chatted, drinking coffee and eating donuts in T-shirts and flip-flops. We spent time together for a bit up front, and then Dad took us to get checked in to the kids' area. He gave the childcare staff our names, and when they asked for birth dates, Dad provided mine and Annabelle's. Then, he said haltingly that he did not know his other two kids' birth dates yet. The new kids were young and did not know them either. The childcare worker looked up and smiled at Dad. Without hesitation, she moved on, printing our tags and walking us back into the kids' area, where she showed us around. She asked Dad if any of the kids might also want a sidekick, another adult volunteer to stick with them one-on-one during the next hour in case they needed anything special. "I think we're good, but thanks. The kids are all happy," Dad responded, and off we went.

When I got to the room with kids my age, it looked quite different from where I had been in the morning. This room *was* filled with kids that looked like my family. Different ages, skin colors, abilities, languages, all together playing, laughing, and learning, with no way to guess who had the same parents. I knew I played rough a lot and questioned everything and talked out of turn and never sat still. After all, I was constantly being told this by adults. But these volunteers were so patient with us all, and we had fun.

My dad had to drag Annabelle out of the kids' area when it ended. She had suddenly decided, after years of fighting it, that she actually loved church and never wanted to leave.

It felt more like home for me, and I think it was more welcoming for my parents too. They tried to sneak out unnoticed after picking us up when the service was finished, but someone in a blue volunteer shirt stopped them; they ended up laughing and chatting for a long time before we returned home. Mom headed straight for bed again.

A few days later, four women showed up at our house with coffee, donuts, and enough homemade meals to last a week—and even some to put in the freezer. Mom got out of bed to talk to them. Though she was quiet at first, when I peeked back downstairs, she was talking and smiling through her tears and then showing them our treasured album of pictures of all the foster kids who had lived with us. I saw them with their hands on her shoulders, praying for her before they left.

One lady had snuck off into the kitchen and had been quietly loading dishes into the dishwasher, quickly handwashing the pile that would not fit in there once she had started the load. The women had figured out what sizes the new kids were and brought a couple changes of clean, folded clothes. That, along with new underwear and socks that fit them, were separated into two shopping bags, one for each of them.

After they left, Mom took a shower. I am guessing she wished she had done that before they arrived, but better late than never. I wonder how they knew Mom would let them in or wanted their help. When I asked Mom, she said she guessed they did not know because she did not know herself, but she was glad they had decided to try.

After that, Mom started feeling better, and my parents went on a date that weekend. Even though the worker who was supposed to fly in and take our two new kids back to Colorado hadn't shown up, the two ladies from the new church we had visited who had offered to babysit for us seemed happy and not worried at all that they had four kids to spend the evening with instead of two.

We never made it back to the other churches we had visited, I guess leaving the way a lot of my siblings had left us. It wasn't a conscious decision. We just kept going back to this evening church until it became our church home. We had many friends there doing what we did. They were also opening up their homes to children who, through no fault of the kids, sometimes had contagious illnesses, cursed like sailors, or told elaborate tales, rejecting every attempt to connect to the adults meeting their needs, punishing their foster parents for caring. I understood now why a few strangers had approached Dad while we were out in public, encouraging him to visit this place. "The people are likeminded," Dad said—it was that simple.

As for me, I no longer felt embarrassed by my siblings' behavior or our chaotic household. Instead, I started to feel like we were understood and were not a spectacle in this new building. And that is how my parents felt too—like they were not alone in their struggles anymore. With the added support and strength, it was inevitable that we would plunge ahead. So, when this weekend's sibling group placement finally did fly back to Colorado a month later, just as excited as they had been when they came, we felt ready for whatever came next.

A lot had happened since we'd become a foster family, and I had turned seven years old by the time we got Star. When Mom received the call for her, it was an easy yes. She was a three-year-old girl, it was her first time in foster care, she spoke English, and there were no medicines to remember. When the transporter called to tell us that she would be late (a courtesy we were almost never given), Dad said no problem and asked if everything was okay. The worker assured him everything was fine; Star was just throwing a fit because she did not want to leave her sister.

"Wait—this girl has a sister?" Dad inquired.

"Oh yes," the worker said casually. "She is seven. We found a group home that will take her. I'll be to you in about an hour."

Dad hung up and approached Mom, relaying the information about Star's sister. "Mmm . . . sad" was all Mom said, shooting Dad a look that said the dialogue was over before leaving the room. Dad followed Mom into the bedroom, and I could hear the discussion they were having get louder even as I turned up the volume on the TV. I did not understand what the fuss was about. We had Annabelle, who was four now, and we had a two-year-old foster sister already living with the rest of us. Wasn't this the boundary?

After some time, Mom came out of the bedroom with Dad trailing behind her. "You're getting two more sisters today, Ben," she said, offering me a weak smile.

I wasn't that surprised. As usual though, a mix of trepidation and eagerness filled me. I quickly reminded myself that whoever was coming to live with us now was more scared than I was and tried to think of ways to help them feel comfortable and settle in. I got out a couple of our bikes and other toys and spread them on the ground while I silently said a prayer that God would help the new girls, my parents, my current siblings, and me with this transition.

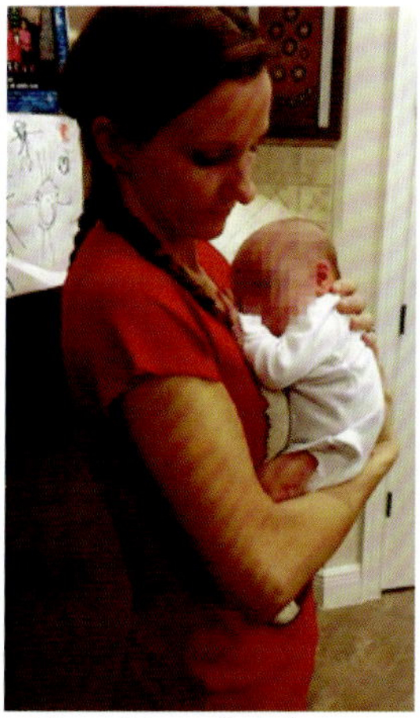

Mom with our first placement.

Dad and a new sibling who arrived late at night. Dad looked perpetually tired but always put on a confident face for us kids.

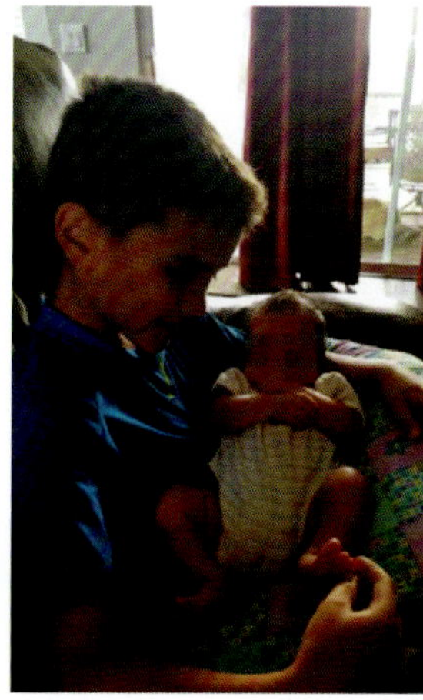

Getting to know a new baby brother.

I always stayed in the back so newer siblings could be closer to our parents.

My parents always let my siblings choose whether they wanted to join in family pictures.

At times, my parents drove two cars to the same place; we didn't always fit in one.

Mom didn't care about messes or stains if we were happy. My sister surprised us by painting herself, and we all thought it was hilarious.

We look innocent heading into church, but we're bringing some chaos.

Heading in to play and have a quick lunch. Heading out after was often a different story.

A like-minded community has been a lifeline for us all since the beginning.

*Dad trying to let everyone cuddle him at once.
Bedtime was a mix of fun and chaos.*

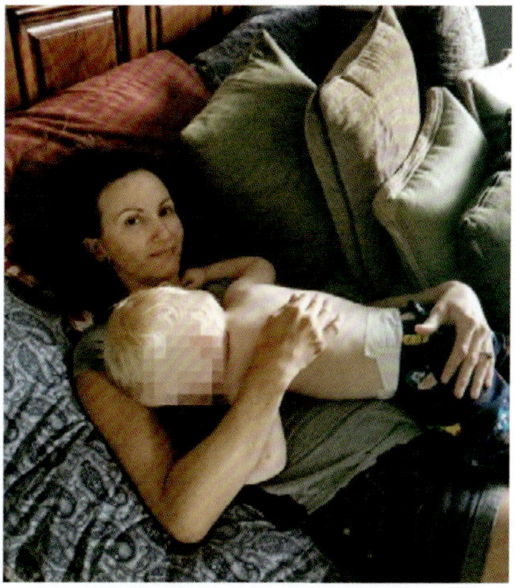

*Mom comforting a new brother and recovering
from a recent loss at the same time.*

Splash pad fun while helping with little brothers.

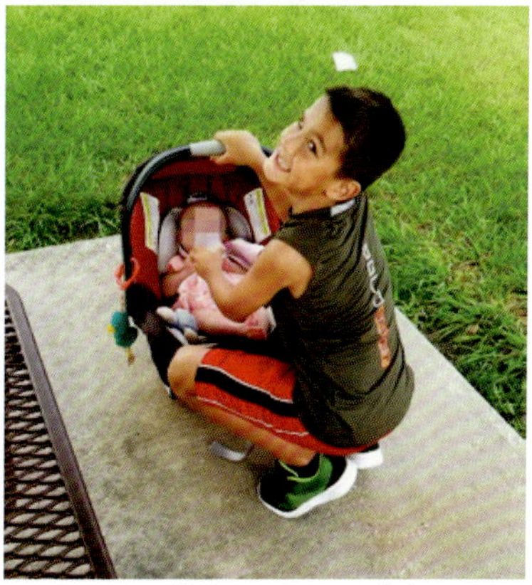

I quickly learned ways to help.

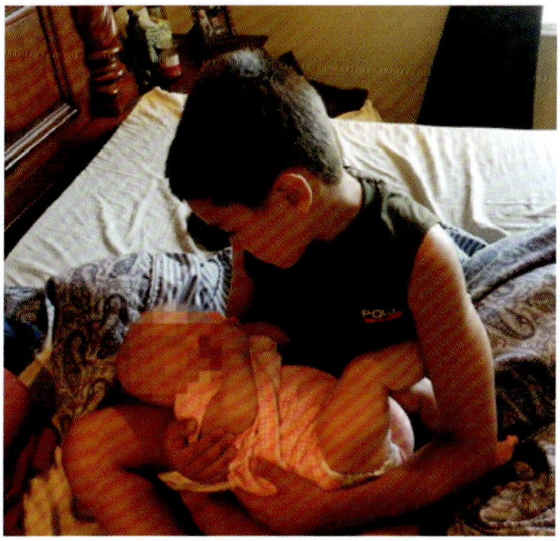

I liked helping with the babies.

Success! I liked bringing home food for us to eat. We ate a lot of venison.

We have had three mastiff puppies. This was the day we went and picked our first one.

Dad was always teaching kids to ride bikes or drive cars.

Goofing off at the beach with a big sister.

Dad's situation when he would get home from work. He was a good sport.

It was fun-filled mayhem trying to get a family Easter picture! We were all laughing hysterically.

We finally got it together—sort of. The dogs always did whatever they wanted.

Summertime fun with a big sister.

Our homemade swimming pool.

It didn't take long to have new siblings to play in our homemade pool with us.

Dad upgraded our pool.

Mom got us bracelets that said "clean slate" to remind us to forgive each other and ourselves.

Respite at the beach.

Summer is almost year-round in Florida, and my family made the most of it.

Fall fun with my big sisters. They taught me how to cook pumpkin seeds on this day.

Results!

Family photos were ever-changing.

Fun beach memories with a big sister.

Mom and sisters playing with makeup on a Saturday morning.

I learned different things from each of my big sisters I have had.

Heading out to go off-roading and witness the start of both my teen sisters' driving lessons.

My favorite sport.

Cornrows after accompanying one of my sisters to her barbershop.

Road trip to the Keys, where we decided to draft a book.

So fun with my dad supporting me.

At the Christian Alliance for Orphans conference, encouraging each other in this work.

CHAPTER SEVEN

WHEN NEVEAH AND Star arrived, I could tell something was wrong. They were scratching their heads and bodies a lot and had cuts and bruises all over them. They were not as shy as I'd expected. To put it simply, I liked the girls right away.

Mom was distracted, figuring out what the girls needed and moving the trash bags they had arrived with back outside after she noticed roaches crawling through the clothes, eagerly trying to escape, when she opened it. Mom needed to get more food for us for dinner too, so after she had quietly set the bags outside to deal with later, she offered to let the girls go with her to the grocery store. Mom said they could point out food they liked and help with dinner. Mom often let us assist with her errands or activities to spend time with us and get her work done simultaneously. The girls were excited to join her, and off they went.

When they got home from the grocery run, the girls offered Annabelle and me some of the candy they had gotten at the store. Of course, we accepted, and we laughed, talked, and ate it even though dinner was almost ready. Mom was being so lenient—or so I thought.

When Mom walked into the room, her jaw dropped. "Where did you get that, girls?" she asked directly. They shrugged and avoided eye contact.

I immediately realized they had stolen this loot. It made way more sense than Mom ever buying candy would, and I wondered if I would go to jail for eating it. I spat out a half-chewed bite of a Kit Kat and tried to declare my innocence, but Mom cut me off. The candy was all collected and discarded, of course, and the girls received a lecture from Dad. He seemed distracted by the end of his talk with them, and after he whispered something in Mom's ear, she looked closely at the girls' heads. It turned out my new sisters were covered in lice, and by now, they were presumably in Mom's car and on her too.

After she had disappeared in the bathroom for a long time and emerged with wet hair wrapped in a tight bun, Mom spent several hours late into the night washing the girls' hair with lice shampoo and combing a tiny lice comb through it. Every few moments, she would drop the bugs into a red solo cup, where they continued to crawl around, desperate to escape, or float in the layer of water at the bottom.

After several hours, everyone went to bed. School was the next day. It would not matter, though, because the school checked the girls' heads as a standard protocol for new students, and Mom had to turn around and bring them home. Mom had missed something when she'd cleaned the girls up.

They stayed home for the next two weeks, with Mom desperately trying to free their hair of lice. Mom made Annabelle wear her hair in a bun so tight it pulled her eyes back. Luckily, Annabelle didn't mind one bit once Mom explained it might help her avoid getting bugs in her hair. Eventually, Mom had to cut Neveah's long hair off, and when that did not help, she called a friend crying. The friend gave her the number for a company that could help, and the next day, there was a lady from Leaving Lice at our house.

The lady was a professional lice cleaner, I guess, but she was still really upset when she looked at the girls' hair. "How did you not notice?" she scolded my mom. "Your daughters have obviously had lice for many months. Why didn't you do anything sooner?"

In a stuttering voice, Mom tried to explain that she had just met these daughters. The lice lady responded with a confused look, of course, and Mom explained the situation in more detail. The lice lady's demeanor completely changed then, moving from shock and outrage to compassion and sadness. She had to come for a few visits but eventually got the job done, and she even checked all the rest of our heads too so that we could stop itching. It turns out the rest of us did not have lice; the lady just called it sympathy pains. It worked—my head stopped itching right away after the girls' hair got clean. The lice lady told me I was clean too.

That weekend, we went to the park to swim in the lake and play on the playground. As it goes in the world of foster families, it was not as simple as it sounded.

When we arrived, Mom sent the girls to use the restroom and then decided she needed to go too. She came out flustered and told Dad that the bathrooms had showers next to the stalls. Apparently, she'd spotted Neveah squatting in an open shower, relieving herself. Mom had been so shocked, she'd fled the bathroom in confusion. Mom said she needed to understand more so she could know how to care for these sisters and would be investigating.

We headed to the lake and all raced in. The water was very shallow where we were swimming, so it seemed perfectly safe. My new big sister, Neveah, crouched down and leaned back to get her hair wet, but she immediately began screaming. The next thing I knew, she was laid out under the surface of three feet of water, flailing. Although she could have easily stood up, her eyes were huge saucers under the surface, and she did not find her feet.

Mom ran out and grabbed her, reassuring her that she was okay. "She got disoriented, Ben," Mom told me when I looked at her questioningly. "It could happen to anyone."

We found out from that incident that the girls had never been to a lake or pool or anything. Mom had them signed up for swimming lessons by the next day. She said we were going to do the same for every brother and sister that came to us from now on, and we did. It was a confusing and stressful day that opened our eyes again to the realities of all that the kids endured before they came to us and how vulnerable they really were.

After the incident, my dad squeezed Neveah into a preschooler-sized life jacket that someone had abandoned on a nearby picnic table, but it did not make any difference. Neveah did not want to go near the water again. We transitioned over to the playground before heading home.

When Mom finally got Neveah and Star's worker to return her call, she looked incredibly sad. We found out the girls had come from an open trailer with plywood on the ground as a bed, bugs and rats scampering around, and, of course, no running water. Seven-year-old Neveah did not use the toilet at home when she needed to go to the bathroom. "It is just not part of her routine," the worker offered. Mom realized the girls were using the bathroom shower at our house to relieve themselves too, so she encouraged Neveah to start practicing on the toilet and put a little toddler potty down for Star too.

By the time she was all set up with swimming lessons, Neveah was ready to pass the school nurse's lice test. Mom indicated she would ride the bus to school, and Neveah seemed fine with that. Dad took her to the bus stop on his way to work, and I rode along since I was getting dropped off at my school, which did not have a bus option, after.

I got out of school before Neveah, and Mom picked me up. Then, we drove to the bus stop and waited. When the bus finally arrived and Neveah got out, she was screaming and running toward Mom, her backpack flapping all over. "I rode the bus with my brother!" she joyfully exclaimed. Mom was very confused, and Neveah repeated herself. Mom did not smile, but she did ask a question.

"You have a brother?"

Neveah excitedly said, "No, I have two brothers, and they ride this bus too!"

Mom went home and made a phone call. "Yes," the worker answered in a bored tone. "They have two brothers who were placed in another foster home."

"Where?" my mom wanted to know.

"Probably the county they came out of when we got them—an hour from you. But I'll check when I'm done driving."

Mom received a text shortly after. *Couldn't find placement together for them all and couldn't find placement for the boys where birth family is so had to move them out to a home in Oakland named the Gonzalezes.*

So, it was true. Neveah had two brothers randomly assigned to a home less than ten minutes away from us, and she was riding to and from the same school on the same bus as her brothers every day now.

Mom said since there were five counties they sent kids to around us, and Neveah's family was not from anywhere near us, the fact that the siblings had gotten split up in DCF custody and then accidentally ended up on a bus route heading to the same school together was a miracle. She was happy and announced we would have to have the brothers over to play soon.

In the meantime, Star had proven not to be as easygoing as Mom and Dad had anticipated. Her anger was like a gathering storm—quiet at first. Brooding. But it would burst open with a force we could not ignore. Still, we all tried to understand her, to connect with her, and we really tried hard not to set her off.

She was very girly, so one time, Mom offered to do makeup and nails with Star, but as soon as Mom turned her head, Star ate the lipstick. She ate a lot of items that were not supposed to be food, but I never saw her get sick. She raged at Mom for taking the empty lipstick tube away, a small section of the "food" she had excitedly ingested hanging from the side of her lips.

It wasn't just at home that she would blow up like that. She would get mad in public over perceived insults like someone walking in front of her. She would pout, scream, furrow her brows, and purse her lips at whoever had inadvertently offended her while we waited out the tantrums or tried to pick her up and take her with us. Meanwhile, curious onlookers would always crane their necks to watch the scene. We never knew what would set her off, but we all knew when she was unhappy.

One day, as a reward for doing our chores well that week, Mom took us out to lunch at Chick-fil-A. It was a new place for my sisters, and they were excited and curious as Mom set down a tray of food in front of us. Everyone got a sandwich and a fry. We all started eating, and Mom asked the girls if they were already done.

"You did not want your fries?" Mom asked.

"I ate my fry already," Neveah said. "You told us one."

"Oh my," Mom replied. "One box of fries, not one fry."

Neveah looked shocked as she moved toward the box of fries as if it were alive. "The whole thing is mine?" she asked.

"Of course, Neveah," Mom said kindly.

It was strange to me at the time. They seemed confused about eating food but were open to eating stuff laying around the house that was *not* food. This memory really stuck with me.

By the time we had finished eating and packed up, Star had decided she loved Chick-fil-A and could not imagine herself anywhere else—she flat refused to leave. Mom tried to gently encourage her, bribe her, threaten her, pretend to leave her—and then finally dragged her kicking and screaming out of the building.

We got halfway through the parking lot, and I thought my level of humiliation was peaking when Star escaped from Mom's grasp. She ran through the busy parking lot, screaming that she hated us. Mom rushed the rest of us into the car and jogged toward Star, but no amount of sweet talking was getting her to leave Chick-fil-A. My little sister picked up pieces of bark and mulch and tree limbs in the grass and threw them at Mom as she closed in. The spectacle was much more interesting to me now that I was safely in the car and could watch it anonymously. Mom ended up diving for Star and dragging her back to the car, with Star managing to rip Mom's shirt and punch her in the stomach.

When Mom shoved her into the van, Star immediately stopped protesting and smiled. "Can we watch TV on the way home, Mommy Michelle?" she wanted to know.

"Sure," Mom said exhaustedly before turning on cartoons for us.

We were pretending the incident had not happened when we got home, and everything seemed to be back on track except for the grass stains on Mom's and Star's clothes and the dirt in their hair.

But as it turned out, Star had not forgiven Mom quite yet for not letting her move into Chick-fil-A permanently. When Mom went into my sister's room that evening, Star screamed at her one last time and hurled her toddler potty that she had just peed in at Mom. It was an accurate shot on Star's part. Now Mom was covered in Star's urine, and in turn, Mom started shaking and burst into tears. In fact, she lost it then, glancing up at the ceiling, letting out a strangled scream, and running to her room dripping wet. I heard the door slam. *Good night, Mom.*

Dad did what he could to clean up the mess and sent us all to bed. I went to sleep that night and dreamed that Star gave me her broken toy, and she wanted me to fix it. I tried so hard to mend it for her. I wanted to help her so badly, and I wanted her to be happy, but there were so many complicated pieces that popped out unexpectedly. The harder I tried, the bigger the mess I made.

I woke up sweating, got water, and went back to sleep. I dreamed again, this time about being stuck in our SUV. It was sliding off a hill under the water, and my parents could not stop it. I jumped up and tried to push the brakes repeatedly, but I could not help this time either, and I screamed in frustration and fear.

I startled myself awake as Mom ran in and put her hands out to me. "Hey, you're okay," she soothed while holding me. "What's going on?" she asked. I explained through tears that I was having bad dreams and told her about them. Mom stared at the bedspread and cuddled me while I talked. Then, she helped me get under my covers and slept next to me until morning.

To my surprise, after Mom took Dad to the front porch for a talk, she came in and said she and I were driving to the beach for a couple of days of rest.

I was shocked and excited for several reasons: I would be missing school, Mom always had tons of other stuff to worry about, and the other kicker—Dad would be staying alone with all the other kids. I packed before anyone could change their mind, throwing swim trunks, shorts, and a toothbrush into a duffel bag.

A few hours later, we arrived at a small hotel on the beach. Over the next couple of days, we collected shells. We ate dinner and breakfast in bed while watching Disney movies. We raced into the cold ocean and snorkeled around. We read books in beach chairs in the sunshine and let a waiter bring us smoothies.

While we watched the waves crash against the shore, Mom and I talked about everything under the sun. We discussed things that made us happy, things we were proud of, and our dreams and fears. I told her I felt guilty because I had so much compared to all the other kids who lived with us. I felt guilty about all the toys and having my own room and eating out all the time and watching movies while other kids my age who lived close to me were going through terrible things. I told her, looking back on everything, I could not believe I had been so worried about sharing my toys when I'd first heard we might be a foster home.

Mom listened, raised her eyebrows with some hesitation, and just said that I was a unique kid. According to her, I talked like a grown-up sometimes, and she felt the same guilt. She then mentioned the nightmares I was having and apologized for not getting me more support sooner. I tried to tell her I was fine, that I knew how incredibly fortunate I was compared to other kids and that she was a great mom. She just smiled at me and listened. She had a way of making things feel better, and I was grateful for the time we had. I knew that no matter what challenges lay ahead, we would face them together.

We went home after two nights at the beach with tanned skin and full bellies. Mom successfully timed it so we arrived after everyone else was in bed. I slept like a baby that night, and she slept beside me again. Early in the morning, she put her hand gently on my forehead for a moment and took a long breath. Then, she slipped downstairs to get back to our real lives.

It took a few weeks before we could track down a number for the Gonzalez family and contact them to have Neveah and Star's brothers over. Even though we had seven seats in the van, we did not have enough space for all the kids to ride together, so Mom and Dad had to drive separate cars and split us up when we went places as a family.

The first thing we did was bring them to our house for a playdate. (Mom had been a little shy about taking the kids out since Star's protest after her first Chick-fil-A experience.) The boys walked into the entryway, and Jake, the ten-year-old brother, walked through the house, followed by Mom, until he stopped dead in his tracks. "There is a staircase in your house?"

"Um, yes," Mom said.

"It's *in* your house though?" Jake repeated.

For Danny's part, he just stood in the doorway and muttered to his sisters disbelievingly, "You live in a mansion?!"

That word had not entered my mind about our house. We did not even have a spare bedroom. I understood by now though why he might have said it. It might have seemed like a mansion compared to the home they had grown up in.

Before anyone could respond further, Jake ran up to his thirteen-year-old brother. "Danny! You're never gonna believe this, man! There is a staircase IN this house."

"What?" Danny asked, confused. He followed Jake to the source of the rumor and stood with his mouth open. "Can we go up it?" he asked.

"Of course," Mom said. "Your sisters' room is up there." But they did not care one lick about their sisters' room. They ran up and down the stairs over and over in disbelief that someone could have constructed such a thing.

When it was time for them to leave, they really did not want to go and begged us to let them stay. I begged Mom to let them stay too. When we had picked them up, it had been obvious to me that their crowded foster home was a harder place to live. They were "over-capped," Mom explained—licensed for two kids but with many more in the home. Dad added that the foster parents were generous, trying to help an overwhelmed system by taking in extra kids who may have had to sleep on a DCF office couch otherwise.

At that moment, Jake's bed was a deflated air mattress in the living room—though, to be fair, he had an air pump plugged in next to it. Jake said his bed would slowly deflate every night, so sometimes, he slept on the couch instead. They ate big pots of rice and beans for almost every meal and were not allowed out of the house except for school due to recent violence in their neighborhood.

Mom and Dad were firm though. We did not have enough seats in the car, but we would do more hangouts together. They also insisted we were wrong about the boys' home; it was suitable and safe and had warm food and access to a good school. Dad explained there were many excellent foster homes with families living close to the poverty line, and there were families who had more resources that would not have been able to offer a physically or emotionally healthy home for kids to stay at. It was the "don't judge a book by its cover" talk, and this was a concrete visual of that lesson for me, one that you could not argue with once you understood what was beneath the surface.

We did drop off a twin bed for Jake so he had more options on where to sleep. My parents explained DCF would have done a home visit and helped with this too, but since we had an extra bed and were nearby, we would go ahead and drop it off to help the family and the DCF workers. The foster parents seemed grateful, and over time, we built a friendship with their family.

Neveah and Star stayed with us a long time. Star was funny, and I liked her, but Neveah and I were especially close. I forgot she might be leaving until Mom approached us after many months and told us we would need to have a special celebration dinner. All of us kids wanted to know why. "Well," Mom said, "the goal for the brothers and sisters that come to live with us is for them to go back home to their birth family. And the girls' grandma got a job at Burger King and a duplex apartment, so DCF gave her permission to take them back!"

However, no one except Mom seemed happy at the thought of splitting up, and I am fairly sure Mom was faking it because she and Dad only smiled when they thought we kids were looking. Nonetheless, we ate pizza and ice cream and talked about how all four brothers and sisters would be living together again soon.

On the day that was chosen for the girls to go home, Mom piled us into the van and picked up the brothers too. We double-buckled since Dad was at work meetings. The brothers were ecstatic to be going to Grandma, but the girls did not seem happy. They were quiet and serious. Mom's voice kept shaking when she tried to talk, but she was working hard to pretend that this was a positive occasion.

When I looked out the window, I asked Mom where we were.

"It's a neighborhood called Drayton," Mom replied.

"Why are all the houses rotted here, Mom?" I wondered. She shot me a look that told me she was not open to answering questions at that moment, so I did not ask all the other questions I had.

"We're here," Mom declared as she pulled up to one of the rotted shacks, half of which would be the new home for my foster siblings. Mom tried to convince us to stay in the car while she ushered in the four kids that would be staying. Of course, I was not going to sit in the car while my sisters left, so I followed them in.

The broken screen door was hanging open, so Mom announced our presence and entered. There were flies buzzing around in droves by the windows and throughout the house, and ants were crawling in lines up the side of the kitchen counter and some of the walls. The grandma was smoking and sleeping at the same time somehow. Mom jostled the woman a bit, and she startled awake, coughing and dropping a long ash off her smoke.

Mom smiled gently at Grandma and said she had brought precious cargo to her. The girls' grandma said she was "fuckin' happy" to see her grandkids and that "there isn't no fuckin' way DCF would steal them again from their kin." At least that was what it sounded like; Grandma had no teeth, so it was a little hard to make out her exact words. I did know all the cuss words she used though; I had learned many of them from Star.

"Mommy Michelle, this looks okay, right?" Neveah asked Mom, who got down low and gave Neveah a hug.

"It looks great, and I am so excited for you to be home with your brothers and grandma. And your mom gets to visit now too." She gave the other kids hugs, and then we left with promises to call and write to each other.

The door had barely closed behind my mom when her tears began silently gushing out. As Annabelle and I climbed into the back of the van, mine would not be held back either. I looked over at Annabelle, but she had put on her headphones and was turning cartoons on her tablet for the drive home. Mom drove around the corner and then stopped the car. Without a word, she put her face down into her hands and cried hard. Then, without warning, she banged the steering wheel with the side of her fist over and over before folding over, her forehead resting on the wheel as she breathed out sharply. It scared me, and I watched through my own tears. Annabelle glanced up briefly, put her hand on her window, and tried to look back in the direction of the house we had just left before going back to her show. Together, we sat in silence for a while. Clearly, Mom's mind was somewhere else.

"Poverty is not a crime, Ben," she finally uttered, but it almost seemed like she was talking to herself. Eventually, she dried her face off on her shirt, blew her nose, and looked at me in the rearview mirror, smiling slightly. "You okay? Let's go home," she said.

But she did not drive off. Instead, she added, "The kids will be okay, Ben. I'm happy for them, and you should be too. It is not a crime to be poor, and it is not an indicator of whether you are a good parent or not. Kids can still be very happy in a home without the extras. I am crying because I think their grandma has had a hard life, and I am hurting for her struggle trying to make ends meet and raise four grandchildren. I am sad that she has a daughter who is struggling with drugs. I am sad that drugs are so addicting and that people who live in certain areas are exposed to them more. I am sad for the kids' mom that she is not able to get off drugs; I know she would love to take care of her kids herself. Addiction is very painful and keeps a grip on people sometimes, even when they are good at heart and really want to stop. I am sad kids must move around and cannot stay in one place, and I am going to miss all four of those kids so much, Ben. And I am scared for them. And I am relieved that I just have you and your sister now, and I feel guilty about that. I guess I'm overwhelmed, and I'm sorry."

I could tell Mom needed me to understand her, so I told her it was okay and suggested we should get some comfort food. She laughed through her tears and agreed. "Tap Annabelle for me, please," she instructed. I tapped her, and she slipped off her headphones and looked up. "Annabelle, are you okay, sweetie?" Mom questioned.

"Yes. Love you, Mommy," she replied quietly, with a small smile.

Mom responded affectionately, her voice wavering. Then, she put the car in drive and pulled out.

We went home, ordered more pizza, and watched cartoons in bed. Dad, who had arrived home from work, smiled into the dark room at us and headed back out to the gym for a workout. That is how he always relaxed and blew off steam, and Mom and Dad respected each other's differences the best they could. I was glad Mom had opted for the pizza and cartoons though.

I stayed close with Neveah and Star and her brothers after they left, and we talked often. My mom had a good relationship with the girls' grandma as well, and she arranged for us to meet at a nearby lake for a playdate after several months had passed. No one talked about the kids' mom though; we knew she was in and out of jail and rehab, still and struggling to get well.

When we arrived at the lake, we were greeted by the joyful and unexpected sight of Neveah's mother playing with all her kids. It was a heartwarming scene that made me laugh aloud with delight, even as a boy. Despite her struggle with drug addiction, it was clear that she was having a good day and cherishing the time spent with loved ones. Her laughter echoed across the water as she gave piggyback rides to her children in the lake. My foster sisters and their brothers were laughing and squealing too.

Then, to our surprise, their mom made eye contact with us and waved us over, offering Annabelle and me a ride as well. I glanced at my mom for permission, and she nodded with a smile. We eagerly ran into the water and hopped on. Annabelle shouted with joy, and I could not help but laugh too as Neveah's mom pulled us around in the water. Neveah and Star joined in on the fun, their laughter blending with ours as we splashed around in the cool water. Even their grandma could not resist being a part of the playfulness. In that moment, we all felt like one big family, united by love and acceptance for each other.

After we played in the water for a while, we walked together on the lake shore, and Neveah, Star, and her brothers and I talked endlessly. All the while, Annabelle was running around next to us and holding the girls' hands. It felt like catching up on years of missed conversations, even though we talked occasionally on the phone. As we said goodbye later, I could not help but feel grateful for the sisters I had gained from this unexpected life we lived and for the extended family that came along with them. Though we have been apart for a while now, these memories remain cherished in my heart and hopefully theirs too.

As we rode home, I thought of how the day reminded me of what Mom had said in the field so long ago—that we're looking for pockets of time that are positive, a refreshing well along the way, something concrete to hold onto in our minds and return to for encouragement when the hard times set back in. I hoped everyone we spent that day with had also drunk from the well of refreshment and put down the hard for a moment in time.

CHAPTER EIGHT

AS TIME PASSED, the weight of my experiences living a life partnered with the chaos of the foster care system began to take its toll on me. My parents grew increasingly concerned about the impact it was having on my behavior and academic performance. I could not seem to help drifting off to sleep in class, failing to turn in assignments, talking out of turn, questioning authority, and coming across as disrespectful. I did not mean to do any of these things; I was trying my best. My mind would just wander, and I got bored so easily. But my pleas were ignored; they decided to act and forced me to see a counselor. I pleaded with them not to make me go, but they would not budge.

Not long after, I found myself sitting on a worn couch across from a grandmotherly woman. She sifted through stacks of paperwork that I assumed my parents had completed before our session. For an hour, she asked me questions and listened attentively. Then, a week later, I returned for another session. Afterward, the counselor requested to speak with my parents alone. As they went into her office with furrowed brows and tense lips, I waited anxiously outside. When they emerged twenty minutes later, they exchanged questioning glances with me before my father cleared his throat and announced that we were going to visit a friend of the counselor. His face bore a look of concern and confusion as he talked. Even the information he presented to me seemed like it was more of a question to him too.

"No way!" I protested loudly, but my parents simply ignored my objection.

Two weeks later, we arrived at the Achievement and Learning Partners building—a place that would turn everything we thought we knew upside down.

I arrived with a packed lunch in hand, prepared to spend the entire day there. I was not excited. As I entered the bustling foyer, I was introduced to a woman named Mrs. Stanton, who greeted me warmly and led me to a cozy room filled with games and books. My mother gave me a tight hug before announcing she was leaving and would return at 5:00 p.m.

Throughout the day, Mrs. Stanton and I played countless games together—puzzles that required problem-solving skills, creative writing exercises, challenging math problems, and memory tests. Her gentle encouragement and genuine interest in me made the time pass quickly and happily. In fact, I found myself opening up to her about my struggles at school and some difficulties at home. By the end of our session, I felt like I had gained a new friend.

I assumed that was the end of my parents' efforts to seek help for me, so I was surprised when we returned to the Achievement and Learning Partners building several weeks later. While my parents met with Mrs. Stanton in another room, I waited nervously in the front room. When they called me back into the office, I eagerly asked if we were going to play more games. However, Dad informed me that we would be having a serious discussion instead. My father began by explaining that Mrs. Stanton was helping us all understand more about me—my strengths, my challenges, and how best to support me as I grew. They showed me papers with combinations of numbers and letters on them, patiently explaining their significance. That was when I received the news: I was "twice exceptional."

I sat with my eyebrows raised while it was explained to me. I was having trouble in part because I was both gifted and learning disabled. My brain was wired differently from others', making it difficult for me to fit in with kids my chronological age, among other challenges.

It was a strange feeling to learn this information about myself, but oddly enough, I felt a sense of relief wash over me. I felt different from everyone around me because I *was* different. And as it turned out, my parents shared a similar reaction of relief for varied reasons. They had been worried that being a foster family might have been negatively impacting me despite my repeated reassurances that I wanted to do it and believed in its importance. But now, we all understood the root of my challenges, and we could work together to overcome them. Now, we all knew there was more to the story. It was like being handed the keys to a new world, one where many of the obstacles suddenly had a roadmap and a toolset to conquer them. I know they wished they had taken the time to figure this out sooner, but at least we were on the right path now.

We all left with our heads spinning and headed back home to our place of rest, a place that also often felt like the trenches with all the unknowns about what was coming next. This one was certainly a shock. Home was a cozy yet chaotic place, and with this latest information, it would soon be filled with even more books and papers scattered everywhere accompanied by the constant hum of life happening. Dad decided we would take a few weeks off from fostering while we worked on finding a plan to help me thrive, and that is what we did.

I was moved up to advanced classes in a new school where my grades improved and I enjoyed learning. Suddenly, I had access to rooms with books stacked high on shelves, a new computer screen glowing with information, textbooks that were thicker, and equations that were more complex. I began to wake up early with my dad and work out next to him—me on the treadmill breathing in the smell of sweat while I pumped my young legs forward, and my dad with his weights, grunting and yelling and wiping his face with a sweat rag at regular intervals. I also took medicine for a while, a small white pill that, along with the colorful schedules and checklists, helped me with ADHD symptoms. I stuck to a routine, learned impulse control techniques, and wrote myself notes when I needed to remember something important. It was a time of profound change and adjustment but also a time of growth and understanding as I navigated my newfound diagnoses and found ways to thrive.

Among the letters and labels that had been attached to me, I learned I had SPD—sensory processing disorder. My family was more understanding of my quirks with food, clothes, and sound, among other things. The result was that I felt closer to my family.

The icing on the cake for me was being enrolled in a weekly impromptu debate competition that I loved even though I was the youngest debater by far. I thrived on the anticipation of the topic I would be given and the countdown of the timer as I made a case for something I had no idea I would be talking about until minutes before I took the stage.

My parents stopped pushing me to play sports and gave in to my obsession with chess. They drove me to competitions and a weekly chess club where adults hunched over chessboards, their hands moving pieces with precision. All the while, my parents would stare at the board and occasionally at me with frustration. I loved it when the games went long, but my parents did not appreciate it nearly as much. They began dropping me off instead of watching me play my chosen sport, even though they had always stuck around to watch when I had played ball instead. Four hours later, they would show back up and give me a ride home, prepared to hear about my chess adventures on the half-hour drive home.

I did not mind at all. For now, in addition to understanding and supporting the brothers and sisters coming through, we all were doing the challenging work of understanding and managing my diagnoses as well. A month passed quickly, and we were ready to get back to work.

And so it went. In the dead of night, while the world slept, Maria and Miguel arrived on our doorstep like so many other children before them. The same age as me, Maria was already hardened by a life of uncertainty and fear. Her younger brother, Miguel, seven years old, clung to her side with wide, terrified eyes.

As for me, I was eight now and had become accustomed to the ever-changing flow of new siblings coming into our home. My mother no longer made me go to bed before these late-night arrivals. Instead, she saw what I saw: frightened children who did not trust adults in their lives. But somehow, they seemed to relax when Annabelle and I offered them toys to play with and showed them their rooms.

Tonight was different though.

CHAPTER NINE

MARIA WAS CRYING hard when she arrived. Her tiny body shook as she struggled to catch her breath. Tears streamed down her face, leaving streaks in their wake and making my own eyes water. Mom got on her knees on the warm asphalt in front of our house, gently pulled this tiny girl into her arms, and held her. She didn't say anything yet, just shared space with her and tried to share the weight of the burden placed on Maria without lying and saying everything would be okay.

I could feel the heaviness of the fear and sadness radiating from her. Gently, I offered her a small smile, and since Mom was not talking yet, I told her simply but confidently, "You'll be okay now." She peeked out at me through her tears, but when I reached out to pat her back in comfort, she jumped back with a startled scream. Clearly, she did not trust me.

Maria was one of those rare siblings who never fully trusted me, no matter how long she stayed with us, but our relationship did grow over her stay. She harbored deep resentment toward men in general, and my father was no exception. My dad could not make eye contact with Maria or walk past her without her bracing herself and drawing back. My mother explained that it was not personal; her cousin, an older boy, had hurt her in the past. She had also lived in a home with domestic violence, so it would be valuable for her to live with a family that was safe so she could learn to trust again. I understood I needed to give Maria space and not take her mistrust personally, just as my dad had to do.

My dad was naturally a loud person who wore hearing aids after years of hunting and mowing yards for work in high school, so accommodating her needs was a challenge for him. He had to learn not to make eye contact with her when he walked into a room, somehow announce his presence before he entered, and talk just above a whisper to keep Maria from getting scared. It was a protracted process of two steps forward and one step back, and Dad was just as frustrated as Maria was scared, but everyone did their best. With time, it got easier. I saw my dad's gentle side as he cared for her by slowing his movements and his voice, proving to the most reluctant young minds that there were some safe and stable men in the world, and he was one of them.

But at this initial meeting, Miguel also glared at me with suspicion and anger as he hung back in our driveway. I offered him a smile and hug—he was so little—but my father quietly pulled me aside and whispered that Miguel appeared to be sick. He told me to put on long-sleeved clothes and pants if I wanted to give him a hug. That was fine with me since Miguel also seemed to want nothing to do with me, except maybe to fight. And soon it was clear that my father was right.

As soon as Miguel entered the house and the entryway lights shined onto him, I could see scabs covering his arms, his legs, and even his face. He could not stop scratching at them. Some of the scabs were raw and oozing with dried blood and dirt. My mother quickly offered him a bubble bath, which he was excited to accept, but under his shorts, she saw the scabs were ten times worse.

My father wasted no time taking Miguel straight to urgent care. When he returned, he brought back a strong-smelling lotion that we had to rub all over Miguel's body every day and taught him to rub it into his skin where his shorts covered. The doctor said he had been suffering from a severe case of scabies for a long time, and it turned out Maria needed the medication as well.

For weeks, the sound of Miguel scratching at his scabs during dinner and the pungent scent of the lotion made it difficult for any of us to eat. We could hear the discomfort and frustration in Miguel's movements, and it was palpable in the air around us. In my dreams at night, I could feel bugs crawling on me and would wake up scratching myself frantically. But nothing brought relief.

It took weeks for the infection to fully clear up, even with the medicine. During this time, my father made us all wear long clothes despite the sweltering Florida heat. Finally, we all breathed a collective sigh of relief as we watched Miguel's scabies, along with the incessant scratching, slowly fade away. Somehow, the rest of our family managed to avoid contracting this terrible skin condition.

Mom took Maria to enroll in school once her skin was clear and we could go out. She planned to drop me off at my school on the way, but shortly after leaving the house, Maria's face twisted in disgust. Moments later, she leaned over and expelled the contents of her stomach onto the floor of the van. Her face was pale and covered in sweat, and her normally bright eyes looked dull. Her mouth remained open in a grimace. Mom pulled over and tried to clean her up, handing her water to try to get the foul taste out of her mouth.

Maria's hair still hung limp and matted when we got home, and she immediately headed to the bathroom to take a bath. Fortunately, she felt so much better after we'd been home for a while that a person would never know she had been so sick. With all the ruckus, I missed school that day.

Mom tried the same route the next day, and the same thing happened. Chunks of half-digested food lay in a pool of spit and saliva as we drove home a short while later. The sharp odor of vomit filled the car, making me gag and stick my head out the window for fresh air. I might have preferred making it to school over all this.

Again, once we got home, Maria's pale cheeks turned rosy, and the light returned to her eyes. She bathed and ran off to play dolls while

Mom and I worked together to clean out the car. It was a task that required gloves and a strong stomach. In the end, the smell of cleaning products and vomit mixed, and Mom left the windows down and the doors open until the unpleasant odor faded.

On the third day, Mom said Maria was nervous about going to school, so she took her to the park instead while Dad dropped me off at my own school in a separate car. But, for the third day in a row, Maria vomited in the van. I smelled it when Mom picked me up that afternoon and instantly knew what had happened.

Mom finally realized the car ride itself was making Maria sick, and she felt bad for not understanding that before. Outside of the ride to us, Maria had never been in a car before, and it took her a long time to get used to riding in one. So, we stopped driving around when we did not have to.

As her older sibling, I had to adjust my own life as well, giving up soccer and constantly being tardy to school because our new route had to accommodate Maria's needs first. Dad could not always drive me since he had to work and drop off Annabelle and Miguel at their school as well. I racked up three tardies quickly, and my teacher took my weekly trip to the treasure box away until I stopped arriving late regularly.

This upset me, but not because I was missing out. The once exciting treasure box prizes at school now held no significance, not when my sister was sick and struggling to adjust to a whole new world that everyone around me took for granted. It made me resent the other kids and their preoccupation with material possessions. My priorities had shifted, and I felt more different than ever from my peers, living with this little girl who needed our love and attention more than any toy or candy ever could.

Just when I thought I could not be any more different from my peers, picture day arrived. This time, Miguel, with his quiet presence, proved to be a source of solace for me.

Picture day fell on a crisp Wednesday morning. Dad woke us all up early and headed downstairs to whip up some breakfast. As he passed by my room, he reminded me that it was picture day at school. "Don't forget to fix your hair, Ben," he said with a hint of urgency in his voice.

I glanced at my reflection in the mirror above my dresser. My hair was slightly shaggy, and I wanted to look sharp for the photoshoot. With a sudden burst of impulsive energy, I grabbed the scissors lying on my dresser and began snipping away at my bangs, envisioning a more stylish and grown-up look. But as soon as I finished cutting off my bangs, my heart sank. They were uneven and too short. Panic set in as I realized there was no coming back from what I had done. Frantically trying to even it out, I cut the sides, which ended up creating bald spots all over my head instead of the sleek look planned in my mind.

My hair was a complete disaster, and there were only a few hours left until picture day. Hair was all over my dresser and the floor. Feeling embarrassed and frustrated with myself, I attempted to use the remaining strands of hair to cover up the mess I had made. But nothing worked.

Then, my mom knocked on my door. "Ben, let's go! What is taking so long?" she called out. Slowly, I walked over and opened the door just enough to peek out at her. She pushed the door open gently, and her jaw dropped when she saw my hair. "What happened?" She choked on her words, trying not to laugh.

"I just wanted to look good for pictures . . . now I can't even go to school," I mumbled dejectedly.

Instead of getting upset or scolding me, Mom hugged me sympathetically but declared that we would stick to our normal schedule for the day. It was time to head to school, and I would just have to eat breakfast in the car on the way.

As we walked downstairs, I avoided making eye contact with anyone. But eventually, they all noticed. "What happened to your hair, Ben?!" my sisters exclaimed in unison, giggling and trying to touch my exposed bald spots. Miguel, usually quiet and stoic, told them to shut up. He smiled at me and suggested with a shrug of his shoulders that brothers should have matching hairstyles. (He had his hair shaved tightly to his head.) In desperation, I turned to Mom and asked if I could get Miguel's haircut. She reluctantly agreed that it was the best option but said it would have to wait until after school.

After surviving an infamous school picture day—it even brings a smile to my own face whenever I come across the pictures now—I finally got my head shaved at Miguel's barber. And to my relief, Miguel declared that I looked "cool" with my new haircut. My sisters loved it too and were constantly trying to touch my hair and rub my freshly shaven head out of curiosity and amusement.

As we rode back home with our matching haircuts, I beamed with pride and enjoyed his reassuring presence by my side. From that day on, Miguel helped me fend off any unwanted attention from girls trying to touch our hair or make comments, and I was more than grateful.

When adjusting to life with us, Maria and Miguel faced so many challenges that it was impossible not to be changed by them. They had never been in a car before, but they also had never experienced other common things that most kids take for granted. For example, once we could drive farther without Maria getting sick, we tried to bring them along on errands, but the pair had never gone grocery shopping before. At first, Maria would cling to Mom's side and hide behind her whenever someone passed by. She seemed overwhelmed by the bright lights and loud noises filling the store. Conversely, Miguel was eager and fascinated.

Slowly, Maria became more comfortable with these routine trips, and eventually, she started to follow me over to the bakery with the rest of my siblings to request a free cookie. Miguel and Maria would touch different items on the shelves and ask what they were for. And when we got home, Maria would help Mom put away the groceries and proudly announce that she knew where everything went. Even something as simple as eating at a restaurant was a new experience for them.

The first time we took them out to eat, Miguel acted like we had arrived at Disney World, while Maria seemed confused and frightened and kept looking around anxiously as if waiting for someone to tell her what to do. With some guidance from us, they quickly learned how to look at the pictures on the kids' menu and even make a request to the waiter about what food they wanted to try.

There were many moments like these—moments when I could see just how different Miguel and Maria's life had been before coming to live with us. I admired how brave and determined Maria was to learn and adapt. I felt foolish for all the times I had been frightened of having a new brother and sister arrive at my house. I realized how much more intense and realistic their fears were. Moving forward, I wanted to take my cues from Miguel, Maria, and other brothers and sisters. I wanted to choose bravery and determination in the face of the unknown.

For months during her stay, Maria kept talking about one thing: she wanted to know why the police would not let her go with her mom. It was a heavy and haunting weight, one that Maria seemed to carry with her always—the scarring memory of the moment her family was torn apart. She kept telling us that she had begged the police and cried, and her mom had cried, but they would not let her stay with her. Maria said her mom had told her only grown-ups could go where she was going. She had tried to hug her, but her mom's hands had been tied behind her back by the police, so Maria had hugged her neck tightly until someone had pulled her off. But this had caused her to accidentally scratch her mom as she dug her nails in and tried to wrap her legs around her so they couldn't separate them. As Maria talked about it, she would clench her fists, and her nails would dig into her palms. The bitterness and fear she felt crept into my own mind as I listened to Maria share this story repeatedly.

Maria often asked about her dad too. I knew he was in the hospital because Maria's mom had viciously stabbed him in the neck inside a cramped, run-down trailer they had found in the woods and called their home. Maria had seen everything play out, and she constantly recounted the story to us. Mom would just say she was so sorry that had happened and acknowledge how scary that must have been before telling her that the doctors at the hospital were so skilled and would help her dad. My mom would also assure her that jail was a place with beds and warm food and helpers where Maria's mom could get help to not feel so angry. I seriously doubted that was totally accurate, but I nodded along with Mom as though I had been in jail and might just return for a holiday myself. It did seem to relieve Maria, and it strengthened her trust and bond with us as we walked through this with her.

At night, because Maria talked about it so much, I would lay in bed imagining what had happened in their trailer, and I understood better why she had been covered in sweat, tears, dirt, and fear when I'd met her. Sometimes during the day though, I would sit with her and all my other siblings while we colored pictures and wrote letters to Maria and Miguel's dad and mom the best we could. We'd include simple phrases like "Feel Better Soon," "You Are Loved," "I Miss You," and "Best Mom Ever." Mom said it would help the kids get all that was inside them out, so even though I wanted to hate Maria's mom, I thought about what might have led to the situation and the violence she herself had endured before lashing out, according to the news stories that had come across my parents' TV. I thought also about what might have prevented it, and showing others unconditional love was one thing I understood could help prevent these things. So I colored and wrote messages to a woman who would later be declared a murderer. I had no idea how to feel. It was hard to grasp that these things happened so close to my own house and that kids my age could ever trust again after living through that.

After several months, Maria and Miguel played, laughed, and ate like they had always been with us. Meanwhile, we found out their mom would not get out of jail, and their dad had died from his injuries.

Maria and Miguel stayed with us a long time as summer turned to fall and then winter. Maria never totally warmed to me, but she stopped holding her breath and tensing up when I came by and eventually just ignored me. When she was reliving something, she often talked about it in front of me, and I took this as a sign she knew maybe she didn't need to be scared around all guys and that some males like my dad and I were safe. Maybe someday she could fully trust again.

Miguel's angry streak always stayed under the surface, but it appeared less and less frequently with time. We had fun together, jumping on our trampoline, playing with water balloons, and riding scooters. However, when I least expected it, Miguel would scream at me or try to hit me or throw something at the wall. In those instances, I would remember his parents and not get mad. I wondered how I would react if he and I were in each other's shoes, and I thought he might be doing better than I would.

Annabelle was much less introspective on the matter and much less empathetic as well. She hit him immediately the first time he shoved her. It took him by surprise, and he channeled his frustration elsewhere after that.

After close to a year, DCF found Maria and Miguel's great-grandfather and his girlfriend. Neither were as old as you would expect them to be. They were willing to take Maria and Miguel in and eventually even adopted them.

The kids didn't want to leave us, and Maria's tears and the look of fear on their faces hit me hard again, just like it had the day they'd arrived, and I cried for them too. After the door shut behind them and we were standing in a quiet house, Mom sat down and cried as well. Dad poured something strong out of a bottle and drank it, then stared at the wall for a minute. After looking quickly at me, he walked toward the garage, allowing the door to slam shut behind him. Annabelle went upstairs and flipped on cartoons until Mom made her head to bed. She held a drawing she and Maria had made together and took it with her, placing it under her pillow.

Miguel and Maria's great-grandpa called Mom that first night, asking for help. Mom comforted Maria and Miguel as well as the great-grandfather. Eventually, they all settled in together.

Mom sometimes shows us new pictures of Maria and Miguel and talks to their step-grandma. Occasionally, we get to see them play in their school soccer league and have lunch after. They have grown up a lot since they lived with us, and their lives are better now. My heart feels happy to know they have family who loves them and will be there for them if anything happens—whether at their house or ours.

Mom said I helped them learn how to trust again and taught them what safe people act like. She explained that I was an important brother to them, even if they did not know how to say that or even realize it themselves when they lived here. I do not know if it is true, but I hope so. I think everyone could use a brother that they can trust and take for granted will be there—one that will not hurt them.

CHAPTER TEN

IT WAS DAD who decided we needed a getaway to recharge this time. He wanted to thwart the sadness Mom was experiencing after Miguel and Maria left. He also loved to fish, and a friend had offered him a free offshore fishing day in the Atlantic, so plans were promptly made.

Early in the morning, just before dawn, we packed bags with snacks, drinks, and hats; slathered sunscreen on ourselves; and jumped in the truck, heading toward the ocean. I was happy, and as we drove, it struck me that this was an experience that my brothers and sisters who passed through would never have had. I wished they could come with us.

Annabelle and I chattered away in the backseat, making bets about who would catch the most fish and how big they would be. Even Mom was excited when we arrived at the marina and swiftly loaded up the boat. As we cruised into the ocean, the sun shone down on us, and we took it all in, enjoying the fresh ocean breeze. The captain, my dad's friend, introduced himself and talked about baiting hooks and casting lines. When we finally launched our fishing lines into the water, the air was thick with anticipation.

Then, Mom spoke up, calling over to Dad, "Honey, my head and stomach hurt pretty bad." I looked back at her and immediately noted that she was not her normal shade. Dad encouraged her to look at the horizon and got her some water, but before a single fish took our bait, Mom doubled over and informed Dad she wanted to get off the boat. I saw Dad and the captain exchange pained glances, but Mom was not budging. She was clearly deteriorating, so we pulled in our lines.

We drove half an hour back to the shore, and Mom struggled off the boat, quickly sitting on a nearby bench. She insisted to Dad that she was fine and encouraged us to keep fishing, so we took off from the marina a second time, eating snacks and chatting, still enthusiastic even if a bit worried about Mom.

We drove past our original spot and eventually tossed our lines back in the water. It was not long before Annabelle yelled in excitement. We rushed over to see what had been caught. It was a big red snapper! My dad cheered her on while she reeled it in, and I used Dad's phone to snap photos. We were all so excited and could not wait to catch more.

For hours, we drifted along, catching several types of fish, including snapper, mackerel, and even grouper. It was exhilarating to feel the weight of the fish tugging on our lines as we reeled them in. My arms ached from the effort, but with the adrenaline rush, it did not faze me at all.

But as we were taking a break to eat snacks and rest our arms, dark clouds began rolling in, and a strong wind started blowing. My dad checked the weather report on his phone and saw that a storm was approaching fast. It happened quickly—before we knew it, big waves were crashing into our boat.

Dad and the captain made a quick decision. It was time to head in. The captain quickly steered the boat toward shore, but before we could reach safety, the storm hit us with full force. The waves were crashing against the boat, and everything was rocking violently.

Annabelle and I felt queasy from all the movement, but our dad seemed unfazed by it all. He was eating snacks and smiling as he watched the waves. Meanwhile, I was getting increasingly dizzy and nauseous and hoped to see the shore soon. I glanced over at Annabelle just in time to see her vomit, making a valiant attempt to lean over the railing, but with the boat rocking, she only had limited success. I moved toward my sister to check on her, but when I got close enough to her to get a whiff of vomit, my stomach lurched, and it was over. I stood next to her and threw up all over the place, which made Annabelle sick again too.

I gripped the railing of the rocking boat and looked at Dad—who was still munching on chips and looking out at the ocean—willing him to notice us. You could tell by the look on his face he was having the time of his life as we battled the rough waters. I yelled his name a couple of times above the storm to no avail. When he finally met my eye, he jumped up right away and came over, helping us both pour water on ourselves and clean up. We were not particularly upset, but our stomachs were on fire. He held onto us, and when we finally reached the shore and the storm gave up and died down to just a trickle, Annabelle half crawled off the boat with Dad's help. I weakly stumbled off behind her. Dad appeared completely fine and was even whistling as he removed our belongings from the boat.

Mom walked around the corner, and a look of surprise hit her face when she saw us. "Are you all alright?" she exclaimed.

Annabelle and I exchanged a glance before I yelled, "This was the greatest day ever, Mom!" My sister jumped in, excitedly telling Mom about the fish she had caught. Mom shook her head with a smile and said she was happy that we were happy.

Dad finished unloading the boat and produced a large, sharp knife, telling us to join him as he walked toward a plastic table under an awning. He expertly filleted the freshly caught fish and explained each step to us. We both got to try our hand at it. The fish's slick scales made it hard to hold, and we laughed at our efforts. When Dad finished, the smell of raw fish and sea breeze filled the air around us. We loaded the meat into the cooler, washed our hands, and left.

That night, Dad grilled snapper. Mom made a lemon butter sauce, and we enjoyed our catch as a family. Mom told us how, after grabbing the book she had left in the car, she had found a coffee shop nearby and enjoyed a lovely day quietly reading and sipping coffee on one of their comfortable couches.

I wondered what Miguel and Maria were doing, and Neveah and her sister and brothers. I felt the guilt creep in again. I was so aware now of having parents around who could take care of me and create fun new adventures and stories to tell. I never had to wonder where I would sleep or who which adults were safe in my home. I understood why some people take their families for granted. I had once done it too, but my life did not allow me that luxury anymore.

Dad set more fish on our plates while Mom laughed as she looked through the day's pictures. We watched a family movie after and then headed to bed, relaxed and refreshed and exhausted all at once. Despite the rejuvenation the day had brought, I couldn't shake the twinge of guilt I could never quite let go of anymore, knowing intimately how fortunate I was.

CHAPTER ELEVEN

IT WAS CLOSE to Christmas and the week after my ninth birthday when DCF called about a sixteen-year-old girl. Mom cut the caller off and said no, our house was not suited for teenagers. The next day, another worker called, indicating the sixteen-year-old girl was sleeping at the office. Could we take her, please? Mom reminded the workers we did not take teenagers, but then again, we could for a night. After Mom reluctantly agreed, the worker thanked us and noted that we needed to be extra cautious because the girl had attempted suicide the previous week and had just been discharged from the psychiatric hospital the day she went into DCF custody. At that news, Mom said never mind—our house was not a good fit for this girl.

The next day, Mom said she could not eat or sleep well. Even though she had said no to a lot of teenagers and slept fine, it was a problem this time. Before Mom could reach out to them, DCF called us again and asked if we could take the girl for just a week so she could get off the DCF office couch. This time, Mom said yes, and Ava was home before lunch. That morning, before Ava arrived, Mom locked up every knife and pair of scissors we owned, hid all our medicines, and even took all our belts away and locked them in her closet.

Before I met her, I was filled with trepidation at the thought of Ava and imagined her angry, swearing, mad at the world. But when she got to us, Ava was kind, smart, artistic, and friendly. She had the same dark hair and eyes and tan skin as me, matched with a curious smile. She had deep scars on her arms that hinted at a troubled past, but other than that, it was hard to tell she needed us at all. As soon as she joined us, Ava immersed herself in our activities. She liked to play basketball and frisbee with Annabelle and me, and we bonded over cooking experiments and laughed together.

At the end of the week, she asked if she could stay. "Of course," Mom said without hesitation. "I was hoping you'd want to do that."

We enrolled her in school, and just like that, she had a fresh start. Well, almost. I had to ride around to many appointments because most of Ava's teeth were riddled with cavities, and she needed glasses to correct her vision. In addition, she needed help with rashes on her skin, and she had a horrible infection that she could not talk about. But after a bunch of trips to doctors, we got to relax more, and Ava could play soccer and swim and run with us more freely.

As time went on, Ava's confidence grew. She did great in school, made friends, learned a lot, and found herself on the honor roll. She helped around the house, and she looked forward to going to church with us. She read and drew pictures, something I could see made her feel free and gave her an outlet to express herself. She told me it brought her inner peace and happiness. She had been living with a boyfriend before she went to the hospital and moved in with us, so I knew our family was a tremendous change. I really loved having her as a big sister. We even went on bike rides together and liked the same foods.

Over the months, I forgot Ava had not always lived with us, and I forgot that she used to be so sad she wanted to die. She seemed to forget too—until, suddenly, everything changed. One evening, the news was playing in the background while Ava was busy talking about college plans with Dad. A picture of a man appeared on the screen, and the news anchor said he had been arrested for assaulting a woman. According to the report, he had been using a drug called crystal meth when he did it. I thought he looked really upset in the picture the police took. Ava's jaw dropped open, and she told us that that man was the guy she had been living with before she came to us. Although my parents tried to comfort her, she was deeply upset and left the living room to head to bed early. For days after that, Ava would Google his name and try to find any updates. She reached out to old friends to ask about his whereabouts, but the answers never satisfied her.

Ava suddenly seemed stuck with one foot in her current life of school, family, and healing and one foot in a life she had tried to forget for a while—one with pain and loss we could not understand. She started slowly bringing up her father's suicide to us—what it was like when she'd found him and how she hadn't believed he was dead and left him lying on the floor until her sister walked into the living room and screamed. She never forgave herself, and as she allowed herself to start thinking about it all, we saw her begin to struggle with anxiety. She had trouble eating, picked at her skin, and only slept a couple of hours a night at times. She wanted to fix her mistakes and did not know how.

Mom connected Ava to a counselor and helped her find some medicine to ease her symptoms, and she spent many hours talking with her. With the encouragement, Ava pressed forward, growing up and trying to figure out who she was while reconciling her past with her present.

As part of that journey, Dad taught Ava how to drive, and she was no natural, although she thought she was. I giggled to myself nervously seeing her behind the wheel of Dad's massive truck as he showed her how to move the seat up and shift the mirrors and pointed out the placement of the brake and the gas pedals.

Ava believed her teenage intuition was all she needed to hit the open road in his truck. She would raise her voice, saying, "I know—I KNOW, Dad!" when he would offer advice or instruction. Based on what I was witnessing from the back seat, Ava clearly did not know what to do without this guidance, but she thought otherwise.

After hearing it for the third time on the way to the movie theater, Dad had had enough. "I'm trying to offer helpful hints on how not to die or kill someone, Ava. Based on the way you're driving, you clearly do NOT know everything!"

He had a point, but that did not stop Ava. She yelled back at Dad, "YOU are going to make us die or kill someone 'cause you keep bothering me while I'm driving!"

I sat in the back seat with my breath held and my eyes big as Dad told Ava to pull over and trade places with him. We made it to the movie theater, and I was happy to get out of that car. You could cut the tension with a knife.

We all enjoyed the Marvel movie Dad had treated us to, but it had to end at some point. Of course, when it did, we were back where we started. Even my nerves were high as we walked back to the car. I climbed into the back seat, and Ava asked Dad if she could drive. Dad did not say anything but raised his eyebrows. After blinking a couple of times and taking a deep breath, he reluctantly handed Ava the keys, the look on his face indicating he was not excited at all about continuing driving lessons.

We almost made it home with no incident—in part because the movie got over late and there were almost no cars on the road. But as we pulled into our neighborhood, we spotted an oversized truck parked to the side of our neighborhood entrance. Ava decided the best way to avoid it was to drive faster, so she gunned the engine. Before Dad could react, we heard a loud bang. When we glanced over, we saw the mirror busted and hanging off the side of Dad's truck.

My jaw dropped, and my heart raced, but Ava was in fighting mode. She slammed on the brakes, rolled down the passenger window, and leaned over Dad's lap to yell out the window. "You hit my car!" she shouted while pointing at the startled man sitting behind the wheel of the parked truck.

Dad told Ava to shut up and apologized to the truck owner, opening the door to pick pieces of mirror up off the ground. Then, he rolled up his window and traded places with Ava once more, even though our house was spitting distance from us by now. "We'll practice again tomorrow, Ava," Dad said evenly as he parked the vehicle and climbed out.

Dad really did take Ava to practice again the next day, and I could not believe his determination to keep helping her after the previous day's disaster. I watched from the porch this time; my mom had decided I should wait a while before accompanying the pair again. I totally agreed with her.

As their driving lessons continued over the next few weeks, I could see a noticeable improvement in Ava's driving skills matched with a reduction of stress covering my dad's face when he arrived back home. Pretty soon, I was in the back seat again, watching as Ava started paying more attention to traffic signs, using her turn signals properly, and checking blind spots before changing lanes. As she grew more comfortable, Ava displayed no more hints of the road rage that had popped up in the weeks before.

One day, as they were practicing parallel parking in an empty parking lot, I saw something I never thought I would see: Dad smiling while sitting in the passenger seat with Ava behind the wheel. "Good job, Ava!" he exclaimed as they successfully parked between two cones without hitting them once. Ava beamed with pride at her accomplishment and thanked Dad for his guidance and patience.

As the lessons progressed to Dad and I relaxing in the car while Ava happily drove us around, I could not help but feel a sense of admiration for both Dad and Ava. From the first day when Ava had nearly destroyed our car to now when she was confidently navigating through traffic, I had seen perseverance from them both, and I was moved by it. Dad never gave up on teaching Ava how to drive, even after their disastrous first attempts. He could have easily admitted defeat and called it a lost cause, but he did not. Instead, he patiently worked with Ava every day, encouraging her and correcting her mistakes until she became a competent driver.

Ava also showed great perseverance in her willingness to learn and improve. Despite initial setbacks and frustrations, she kept coming back to practice with Dad and never gave up on herself. She eventually took Dad's advice seriously and worked hard to correct any mistakes she made. Both Dad and Ava showed me that with determination and persistence, anything is possible. They also taught me the importance of patience and having a positive attitude in the face of challenges.

As their lessons ended and Ava finally received her driver's license, I felt proud of them both. They had not only accomplished their goal of teaching Ava how to drive safely but had also displayed great tenacity despite the roller coaster that driving lessons had been. Ever since that day, whenever I see someone struggling or facing obstacles in their path, I remember my dad's words: "Perseverance is key." And I know that with hard work and determination, a person can overcome all kinds of challenges, just like my dad and Ava did.

The following week was business as usual, and all of us went to school. After school, Mom picked Annabelle and me up before heading to Ava's school. The administrator kept radioing for Ava because she had not come out for pickup. Mom pulled out of the car line and waited. After a while, the principal came out. With a grave expression on her face, she said that Ava was gone. They had just seen on the school's surveillance video cameras that after first period, she had left in an old car with another teenager, carrying a duffel bag along with her backpack.

"She's gone?" Mom was shocked.

Annabelle screamed "AVA!!!" from the back row of our SUV. I think everyone had forgotten she was even in the car. That's when Mom realized she needed to keep it together. "Thank you," Mom said mechanically to the administrator before driving off.

We went to Panera Bread and sat in heavy silence. Mom got us some comfort food in the form of mac and cheese and chocolate milk while we tried to process what was going on. The smell of freshly baked cookies filled the air, but the usually heavenly aroma made me feel sick.

My sister had left? I did not understand at all; everything had been going so well. It was almost Christmas, and she had presents under the tree. We were planning to bake cookies together that weekend. Maybe she was just skipping school? But she had never done that; she would have returned before school was over. And she'd had a duffel bag with her.

I was desperate—I knew we had to find her. God had brought Ava to us, so she could not leave now like all the other kids had—so suddenly and with zero warning. Not this time too. I wondered what I could have done to prevent her from leaving. Maybe she was sick of me. Maybe I should not have hugged her so much or bugged her to play soccer with me.

Annabelle stared quietly at her food but said nothing. I could tell she was just as upset as me just by glancing at her.

Mom's phone buzzed; Ava had sent her a message. I could see the pain etched onto my mother's face as she stared at it. Her hands had just stopped shaking when the message came through, but at the sight of the incoming text, her trembling started again. I felt dizzy watching Mom. Ava's message was simple: *I'm sorry. I needed to help a friend. I'm safe though. Thanks for everything.*

I saw Ava's face in my mind, her bright eyes and her contagious smile. *I need you, Ava*, I thought. *We need each other.*

But that was it. Mom said she was turning eighteen in a couple of weeks, and we must let her choose her own path. She also tried to explain to me that Ava may be trying to heal her past by helping this troubled friend now. I knew she was talking about the guilt Ava held onto about her dad's death. I also knew this wouldn't bring him back or help anything, but what Mom said was true. Ava was turning eighteen, and we had to respect her right to choose her own path.

Ava's absence left a void at the dinner table, and her Christmas presents under the tree were now a painful reminder of her departure. We had already taken pictures for Christmas cards and sent them out. Mom always let the kids living with us decide if they wanted to be in our pictures with us. Everyone wanted to, and Ava was no exception.

So, I saw the happy Christmas picture of her, Annabelle, and me together when I went to our neighbors' and friends' houses for weeks after that. Eventually, Mom quietly removed all her presents from under the tree and gave them to other foster teens' parents to give to their kids. I wanted to save them in case Ava came back, but Mom said we had to let go. Her clothes were still here, her pictures were still on the wall, and her memory was still etched in my heart. How was I supposed to let go? I cried bitterly.

When I would not stop asking them about her, Mom and Dad finally explained she had helped bail out of jail the man we had seen on TV, and she was choosing to stay with him now. Nothing made sense anymore, especially being a foster brother. For a long time after that, sadness dug grooves into my parents' faces when we came across a memory of Ava.

It turned out though that we would see Ava again. Every so often, we would travel a couple of hours to meet her for lunch or to help her with her kids. Ava had three kids of her own in the following four years, and sometimes, she would go to jail. Even still, Ava will call Mom, who will sneak out onto the porch to listen or to talk, depending on what Ava needs. I have stayed connected with her over the years too, and sometimes, we get to hang out or video chat with each other.

It is harder for me to recognize Ava now; she has changed so much. I will never ask her, but I often wonder whether she regrets leaving. Mom says the important thing is that we are still family for Ava—that we love her unconditionally and keep answering the phone when she calls and visit her when she wants us. That is not hard; after all, she is my sister.

After Ava left, it was Dad's turn for a much-needed getaway. Since it was hunting season, we were both in luck—Dad was finally taking me hunting. I had been target shooting for a while and dreaming about the father-son road trip up to Georgia. Finally, it was time. As we loaded up the gear, Mom and Annabelle milled around, making plans for a movie night at home and wishing us luck.

Dad and I set off and drove the six hours with only one break. I slept on the way, bored by Dad's nutrition audiobook, and woke up as we got off the highway. We stopped by Grandma's—Dad's mom's—house and had dinner with her. Then, we set off for the farm, where we would hunt. Once we arrived, we settled into the cozy cabin and went to bed early, excited for the next day.

Dad shook me awake well before dawn and told me to get dressed. I was groggy and disoriented, but as soon as I remembered where we were and what we were doing, I shot out of bed with excitement. Dad had already laid out my hunting clothes, a thick camouflage jacket and pants, along with insulated boots and gloves. He had brought some for himself too, but he was already wearing them.

As I quickly got dressed, Dad started to pack up our gear for the day. Then, we headed outside into the chilly morning air with just enough light from a tiny flashlight to make out the silhouette of the trees surrounding us. Dad led us through the quiet farm, softly pointing out different landmarks and explaining where we would be setting up for the day. We climbed into the stand, and he gave me a quick refresher on gun safety before handing me my rifle.

As we settled into our blind for the morning, Dad reminded me how to dial down my scope to look for deer in the distance. It was peaceful sitting there with him in silence, just waiting for our prey to come by.

After an hour or so had passed without any luck, Dad pulled out a thermos of coffee and one of hot chocolate and poured us each a cup. We sat there sipping our drinks until we spotted a doe in the distance. Dad quickly grabbed my cocoa, helped me set up my shooting position, and reminded me of all the steps we had practiced while target shooting: proper stance, breathing technique, slow trigger pull.

My heart raced as I aimed at my first deer ever and very slowly squeezed the trigger, surprising even myself when the rifle blast came. The deer dropped instantly, and Dad let out a whoop of joy.

He congratulated me on my shot, and after making sure the safety was back on the gun, we climbed down from the stand.

After taking a couple of quick pictures, he began field dressing the animal with efficiency. As he worked, he explained each step to me in detail so that I could learn how to do it myself one day. Once all was said and done with the hunt, we headed to the meat processor for some assistance finishing the job and then drove back to Grandma's house. She was happy for us and warmed up some lunch. We filled our bellies with fried chicken and lima beans and then sat in the living room chatting. I dozed off since I had been up since 5:00 a.m.

A brief time later, Dad's phone rang, and he answered it on speaker, ready to share the details of our morning success with Mom. But as he said hello to her with a big smile on his face, we heard her cry out. "She's dead, Ben!"

Dad's face dropped, and he jumped out of his chair, simultaneously taking the phone off speaker. "What's going on?" he demanded.

"She's dead! My mom killed herself."

"Slow down, Michelle," Dad insisted loudly.

My grandma tried to encourage me to leave the room with her, but I ignored her. I was terrified by now and wanted answers.

"I think she died of a drug overdose," Mom continued. "My grandma just called me and told me, although she said she didn't know how it happened. The police visited her earlier, and she's letting the family know now."

Dad responded, "Okay, we're heading home right now. I am so sorry. But Michelle, you knew she had a serious opioid problem, and I know you two had not talked in a long time. Is this really that shocking?" Dad sometimes did not have a way with words.

Mom hesitated, questioning herself. "I guess I just cannot believe she is dead," she finally stuttered in disbelief. "It's permanent—she'll never get better now." Mom started crying again. "I'm going to call her roommate and find out what happened," she told him.

We drove down from Georgia to Florida just as quickly as we had driven up the day before. Mom's life had been complicated, to say the least, and the person she always referred to as her mom was actually her birth mom's twin sister. This aunt had raised her from a baby until sometime in elementary school, and Mom had moved back into her house as a teen too. Mom credited their relationship as being one of the reasons she wanted to foster children in need. Mom wanted to pay her kindness forward.

When this mother figure developed a dependence on opioids after a minor surgery, it had pained Mom to witness the change in her, and she had tried to help, driving her to rehabs and hospitals and even up to Pennsylvania from Florida in an attempt to establish a new environment for her. I know Mom had hoped someday this mother figure would heal and be able to reconnect. Now, that would never happen.

Mom was still inconsolable when we got home. We found her lying in her king-size bed, crying face down into the pillow. Dad took off his shoes and lay down on one side of her, and I spread out on her other side. Dad put his hand on her back, and I hugged her around her waist, burying my face in her sleeve. Her tears and breathing slowed after a while, and Dad suggested we get out of the dark and go for a walk. Dad had sent a friend to get Annabelle, so it was just Mom there, and the house was dark.

Mom was too drained to argue; she sat up and moved slowly toward her closet to get a jacket. She did not return though, and when we investigated, we found her lying on the closet floor crying again. Dad tried to encourage her to no avail. Finally, he leaned down and stuck his hands under her armpits. Swift as could be, he picked her up off the floor like she was a little child and stood her up. Before letting go, he said firmly to her, "Stand up!" Mom did stand up then, and we left on the slowest walk we had ever taken. I guess the fresh air did help Mom because she drank the soup Dad heated up when we got back and then went outside to return some missed calls from her family.

I knew that some of my foster siblings had parents with the same opioid problem, and it confused me that my family was going through the same thing. Watching how drugs had damaged so many lives around me, I vowed never to fall into their trap. I saw firsthand how drugs could destroy a person, and I knew from an early age that I could never see it casually.

Of course, the fact that many of my foster siblings had been removed from their homes due to their parents' drug use was largely responsible for my resolve. Watching them cope with the trauma they experienced was heartbreaking. Just as significantly, I understood these moms and dads were good people with their own hopes and dreams, watching their own lives fall apart as they struggled to break free from this monster.

But now, watching my mom's family go through turmoil because of her parent's addiction opened my eyes even more to the destructive power of drugs. It showed me it happens in all social classes, all educational statuses, and all types of family units.

As I got older and looked back on this experience from a more mature perspective, my resolve to stay away from drugs renewed. I knew how easy it was for a person to fall into addiction and how difficult it was to break free from its grasp. The idea of losing control over my own life and becoming dependent on a substance terrified me. I promised myself I would never accept any medication unless it was truly necessary. I did not want any substances controlling my life or changing who I was as a person. This one felt like a hard lesson learned over and over.

CHAPTER TWELVE

EVENTUALLY, MOM'S GRIEF subsided, and my parents started answering their phones again for placements. Three weeks after I shot my deer and raced home to Mom, we got a call for a sibling group of two kids. The boys were six and nine. I was ten. Chrome and Trace showed up at night. Why everyone seemed to arrive at night, I do not know; it was just the way it went. Annabelle was asleep by the time they arrived, but I almost always stayed up now when we got new kids, and tonight was no different.

"Wow, you're big for being six years old," Mom commented.

"I am not six," he laughed at Mom. "I'm five!"

Mom raised her eyebrows and smiled but did not say anything.

They were hungry, which Mom had anticipated, so she had already set out chips and cheese dip and apples for them to snack on. But I could tell there was a problem. Both kids talked awkwardly, as they each only had a couple of broken chunks of black teeth jutting out of their gumlines. When they moved toward the kitchen, she pushed the food she had set out into the corner and offered them chicken noodle soup from a can. Mom quickly warmed up the soup and served it to them before stepping into the other room to look through their paperwork.

I followed her. "Mom, why didn't you give them the snacks you made up in the first place?"

"Buddy," Mom replied. "You saw the kids don't have many teeth. I didn't know if it would hurt for them to try to eat that food, so I warmed up the soup." She shrugged. "Also, I have Trace's birth certificate here, and he is six, turning seven in two weeks. We should tell him."

This was a new one even for us, and as we watched the kids rapidly finish their soup, Mom walked over to Trace with his papers. Although I was fairly sure he could not read, she showed the birth certificate to him anyway. "Look, honey. Right here it says the day you were born, and guess what? You turned six almost a whole year ago! In two weeks, you will be seven."

She said this with a gentle smile, but Trace sprayed soup everywhere when he shouted back at her, "I'm SIX?" He was not upset though—he was happy. "I'm six!" he proudly announced to his brother and then to my dad and to me with his toothless grin.

Mom relaxed and smiled big. "Yes, you are. How wonderful—you are growing up. We will celebrate!"

We went out for ice cream the next day, presumably because it was easier to eat without teeth compared to some of the other options we might have gone with. Annabelle was accepting of her new playmates and happy about the ice cream, and she sang "Happy Birthday" to Trace through a mouthful of dessert. Everyone enjoyed it, and we visited the science museum after to play. We all had a wonderful time there too, except my mom dealt with something that came up a lot.

"You need to brush your babies' teeth better. Why do you let them cuss like that?! Teach them some manners!" a woman exclaimed loudly to her. Mom just smiled and walked away. "You're neglecting your children. You're lucky I don't call DCF!" the woman called threateningly after Mom.

My parents were often blamed for the injuries and behaviors that came along with the new brothers and sisters that arrived at our home. And even though the rotted teeth, wounds, and outbursts should have brought empathy from strangers and an awareness that life had been hard on my new siblings, it produced anger and judgment as well.

I would get defensive and angry, and repeatedly through the years, Dad had to remind me, "It doesn't matter who strangers blame, Ben. If we kept our eyes on the world's judgments of us, we would not be taking in foster children in the first place. It looks crazy from the outside. The people who know us well—the people we do life with and share our struggles with—are the ones whose opinions matter. In some ways, the world not understanding us may even be a sign we are on the right track. I am not sure it is better for our hearts or minds in the long run to play it safe. Anyway, let's schedule a hangout with our community group this weekend."

And so we did. We swam in our friend's pool together and had a bonfire. The parents laughed, and the kids played, and we could set down our guard and just be a real family, making memories and sharing life together with like-minded people.

After Chrome and Trace had been with us for a month, DCF came to visit. It was a busy week since we were also doing respite care for another family and had a third placement with us, a seven-year-old boy. Our respite placement showed up vomiting and with a fever, so we were tired and a little overwhelmed even without the DCF visit.

Put simply, we had a complicated relationship with DCF. We loved the workers but struggled with the system itself, and we knew the workers had one of the toughest jobs with a high turnover rate. Dad had talked about this several times when plans got canceled or kids left us with no warning. Still, we befriended anyone we could.

Today's worker was new—an extremely petite Hispanic woman who was all business. After the formalities, she asked to see my siblings' room to take a picture. I led her upstairs, and she looked across at me, briefly taking in my cowboy boots and camo tank top and jeans. Then, she glanced at the room and exclaimed loudly to me, "You have a trundle bed in here!"

I just stared at her, not sure what direction we were heading. Mom walked in and raised her eyebrows, explaining it was a permanent bed that one of the teens that lived here had chosen herself for the room.

"Yes, but it has another mattress hidden underneath, doesn't it?" the worker pushed.

Mom had worried when we'd let my older foster sister get the bed whether DCF would pull up the guidelines against trundles and protest, but she had given my sister the freedom to choose and followed through with her promise. "It does have a hidden mattress that pulls out," Mom admitted. I braced for the reprimand, but it did not come.

"So, you have an open bed in here then! You only have three kids in this room and one open mattress! I can let on-call know there is an open bed here!"

My eyes were saucers now, and when I glanced up, Mom's were too. "No, please don't do that." Mom laughed nervously. "I honestly do not even have that many spaces in my vehicle."

The worker turned her palms up toward Mom and grinned enthusiastically. "That's okaaay," she replied in a chipper tone. "Your husband can drive some of them in his car, and you can drive some in your car. You have two cars, right?"

Mom smiled. "We do have two cars, but I have only one body and one heart. And my heart is overwhelmed at the moment. I want to help, but I cannot take in any more kids right now. I'm sorry."

The worker tilted her head and smiled acceptingly, promising she would check back soon in case anything changed. Mom chuckled and narrowed her eyes at the worker playfully but did not say anything else.

The worker headed out, and as soon as the door closed, I threw up all over the floor. I guess I had gotten what the new kid had. Mom cleaned it up and put me to bed with a bucket. "One day at a time," I heard her mutter to herself.

Chrome and Trace's dental repairs were completed by the time they were transitioned back to their family. My dad drove the kids to many appointments, and eventually, they had their old, black, broken teeth out and new, white, whole teeth in. Dad gave their great-aunt and -uncle all the paperwork and the new Medicaid card, including the instructions on the next steps to keep Trace and Chrome's teeth healthy. I could tell Dad was a little nervous about how to approach the situation since their relatives' teeth looked like the kids' teeth had before they had been repaired.

Trace left with some extra toys and clothes since we had gotten to have a six- and seven-year-old combined birthday party for him before he left. With his new teeth and understanding of his true age, he now carried himself with pride and confidence when he walked. It was wonderful to see.

As I watched the boys pull out of our driveway, my heart ached over the stark contrast in their lives over such a short period of time. Both of the kids' grades at school had shot up from F's—since they'd rarely attended—to B's and C's, which were proudly hung up on the refrigerator. The anger and irritation that had followed them around when they'd first arrived had dissipated, and Mom explained that being in chronic dental pain would have caused anyone to be irritable. But how could a kid almost my age not even know his own birthday?

Frustration, anger, and fear for them started to well up inside me until I reminded myself of the conversation my parents had already had with me about this. They explained that their mom lived in a remote and impoverished area with little access to resources or support. She herself was battling a serious medical illness, and despite her best intentions, she simply could not give her children the care they needed. She was in and out of the hospital, had to try to get to something called dialysis every week, and could not work or take Chrome and Trace to school regularly, as much as those simple things may have been a dream of hers. It was a difficult reminder of the harsh realities that some families face. A woman who dreamed of being able to work and drive and take her kids to school, the very things we groaned about.

It affected my parents too, and we talked about how to help provide support and resources for families like theirs so they could stay together. The very first step we felt was seeing these situations through a compassionate lens. Connecting with organizations whose goal was poverty alleviation could provide more concrete ways to help too. Community support could change lives, so stirring up others' awareness of what was happening in their communities and trying to increase involvement was an idea we had discussed.

The issues were complicated though, and it felt overwhelming to me at such a young age. That day, I just saw brothers pulling out of our driveway forever with a lot of unknowns ahead of them, and it hurt.

CHAPTER THIRTEEN

A FEW DAYS later, I rolled out of bed on a Saturday morning and heard my family chatting in the kitchen. It was a couple of days after the boys had left, and I was still feeling a little down about it.

Suddenly, Dad's voice boomed through the house. "Kids, get dressed and meet us in the kitchen. We're going on a field trip."

I threw on some sweats and ran downstairs to find our parents waiting for us in the kitchen. Mom handed us each biscuits for breakfast while Dad explained that we were going on a surprise outing. Annabelle and I begged them to tell us where we were heading, but they just smiled mysteriously. We piled into the car and drove for an hour until we pulled into a large farmhouse on several acres of land.

There were dogs running around everywhere, barking and playing with each other. Annabelle and I immediately jumped out of the car and ran toward them, our parents following close behind. These dogs were huge, and there were so many of them. There was a hanging sign that read "Gentle Giants," and that described them perfectly from what I could tell.

Dad stopped in front of a large, fenced area where some puppies were playing together. "So, have you figured out the surprise?" he asked.

"We get to play with the puppies today!" Annabelle yelled.

Our parents laughed, and Dad said, "Yes, and we will be taking one of the puppies home with us too. They are called English mastiffs."

My mood was at an all-time high now—I was so excited! I asked Dad if I could help pick out the puppy, and he said that was why he had brought us—he wanted our help. We spent some time playing with the puppies under the watchful eye of their mother before making our final decision on which one to make part of our family. As we drove back home with our new puppy, we could not stop smiling and talking about all the fun adventures we would have, trying out different names for our gentle giant.

We quickly fell in love with our new puppy and laughed often at his playful antics. It was amazing to see how fast our puppy, Noble, grew. In the first year he was home, he grew to over two hundred pounds! Despite his size, he was the sweetest and gentlest dog you could ever imagine. He loved nothing more than cuddling up on the couch with us or playing fetch in the backyard. We took Noble everywhere with us, including to the local farmers' market on weekends. People were always amazed by his size and would stop to pet him and take pictures with him. He was a hit wherever we went.

One of our favorite memories with Noble that year was playing in the sprinklers together on a scorching summer day. At first, he was not sure what to make of them, but soon enough, he was chasing after the water and rolling around in the grass. It was so much fun, and Annabelle and I laughed until we lost our breath.

Later, when Christmas approached again, my parents surprised us with an outing to Bass Pro Shop. They allowed dogs inside, so we loaded up our gentle giant and headed there. We were ecstatic to bring him along with us, and it turned out to be a fun Christmas memory. We even took a picture with Santa Claus—all three of us together.

Noble would stick close to me at times when I was feeling sad about troubles we had at home. He would sense it and come snuggle up next to me, comforting me with his warm presence. In quiet moments, he was by my side. Sometimes, I would sit in our yard under a big oak tree by our playground to get some silence and reflect on everything our family was going through. He would lay next to me, offering silent support and understanding.

My furry best friend was one of the highlights of my childhood; he brought so much love and happiness into our lives during a time that was constantly twinged with uncertainty and confusion. Noble did not like hurricanes though, so we fed him some Benadryl and kept him comfortable during the Florida storms.

One hurricane that passed through brought us another teenager.

We got the call for Kenya a few hours before the hurricane was anticipated to close in on us. She had been on one of the last flights in before the airport shut down. When the call came in, we were just finishing up preparing for the coming storm, and it was safe to assume no one would be coming or going from our house for a while—or so we thought.

The worker that reached Mom said that Kenya was about to land at the airport and our house was closest. "We are trying to get her to a safe place before the hurricane hits," the DCF worker explained. The girl was eleven and was a human trafficking victim coming in from Belize after being trafficked to tourists there. "I promise this little girl will not be any trouble at all, and I can drop her off myself." She sounded desperate. "Kenya's dad is here, and we are going to try to reunite them soon." The worker went on to explain she may not speak English, and they did not know anything about her.

Mom and Dad quickly agreed: "Okay, bring her over."

Preparing for the hurricane turned into us preparing for Kenya. When she arrived, she looked like she was sixteen. Once Mom had established Kenya understood some English, she commented to Kenya that she looked so old to be only eleven.

Kenya looked confused. "I'm fourteen years old," she said.

Mom paused and then nodded and smiled. "That makes more sense. The worker we talked to on the phone must have gotten confused." Dad glanced at Mom a bit skeptically but didn't chime in.

Kenya slept a lot and pulled her hair out all day. She had no eyelashes or eyebrows already, but she incessantly picked at the hair on top of her head, leaving bald spots. Mom tried to help her quit, and Dad complained about all the hair curled up on his computer keyboard after she used it. Mom explained it was an anxiety problem and that we would not be able to solve it over the weekend. We would just have to let it go for now. Dad begrudgingly stopped bringing it up, but I could tell he really wished she would just stop. If only it were that easy for Kenya.

The hurricane passed through with us all hunkered together in a hallway closet, where we slept, tossed, turned, and got startled awake by the high winds and branches hitting the window. But it did pass eventually, and a couple of days later, DCF came to pick up Kenya and take her to her dad. We were happy that she would be reunited with him, but Kenya was not so pleased. "I don't want to leave. Can I please stay here?" she wheedled.

Mom looked concerned about the way Kenya was feeling, but DCF hurried her into the car. I saw Kenya's eyes fill with tears, and it disturbed me. I glanced at Mom, who I could see was equally distressed but trying to smile through it. Why was Kenya begging not to be reunited with her dad?

We went back inside our house feeling confused. Her placement with us had been such a whirlwind, but still, we cared for Kenya's well-being. My mom sat down at the kitchen table with a cup of tea, her face reflecting the same sadness that I felt. She breathed in deeply, looked at me, and said, "We did what we could for her. We provided her with a safe place and showed her love. That's all we could do."

I nodded, understanding what she meant but still feeling helpless. We prayed that Kenya would be safe and slowly tried to get back to our routine.

CHAPTER FOURTEEN

IN JANUARY 2020, when I was eleven years old, Mom took us to Home Depot to buy paint. We carefully chose the color to repaint Annabelle's homemade bed, looking through piles of what others saw as assorted colors, all of which I personally would have called "gray." Once we chose the perfect gray for us—one named "Fossil River"—we walked down the aisle for the face masks to avoid fumes. The whole wall was bare though.

An employee walked by, and Mom asked them if there was somewhere else she should look for them. "Oh, no, don't bother," the man said. "Someone came in here and purchased them all and said he was sending them to China." Mom tilted her head and looked inquisitively at the employee. He shrugged and walked off. We rarely watched the news, and if coronavirus was being discussed at that time, we sure did not know about it. Without another thought, we went home and dragged the bed outside where Mom painted it. However, it was not long after that we started to understand what the man at Home Depot had been referring to.

My dad stopped going to work, and my sister and I stopped going to school. Well, not totally. Mom helped us with our studies at home, and we did art and exercised every day. We could not go out for anything though, and eventually, I started having a tough time getting out of bed. I even quit eating as much. I did not see anyone outside my house and had no plans for the near future. Sports, camps, going to work with Dad, friends, school—everything was gone suddenly.

Mom told Dad she thought I was getting depressed, and that is when we started breaking the rules and going out anyway. We would head to the skate park, go to the grocery store, and drove to visit with more of my extended family and friends at a beach house. Dad started leading family Bible studies regularly and taking us on long walks and bike rides. My parents often talked fervently in hushed tones, and I could tell they were trying to figure out how to handle this new situation, all the contradictory information they were receiving, and news of friends coming down with the illness without worrying us.

We knew COVID-19 was affecting the fostering community in a big way too, and we were trying to figure out how to respond. The support that families—both biological and foster—usually received through after-school programs, in-person therapies and counseling, sports, and other outlets was suddenly gone. Parents lost their jobs, and lack of income became a stressor. Even public parks technically shut down, and of course, gyms and other group exercise stopped. As a result, people's physical and mental health suffered, regardless of their age. At the same time, adults like teachers, coaches, and DCF workers who were usually checking on kids were no longer seeing them in person, and kids who were in schools that had shut down no longer had the breakfast and lunch they would normally receive. Court proceedings that would lead to adoptions and reunifications of children with families were delayed, and even the recruitment and training of new foster families slowed down.

We had put a hold on our foster care license just before COVID hit for a respite from all the transitions. So, we began focusing on providing breaks for foster families we were friends with, taking their foster and adopted kids in for a few days while the parents had a restorative vacation alone, moved houses, or got over an illness. Although I'm sure the adults around me would probably disagree, I remember this period as being more relaxed since the kids were only here for short periods of time, the adults connected to them were thankful and trusted us, and most of the time, we knew the families already.

One day, when he was leading our family Bible study, Dad shocked us by saying he felt like we should adopt. Mom and I both glanced at each other and chuckled since the one thing Dad had said from day one of fostering kids was that the goal was always for us to help them get back to someone in their biological family. Any time Mom and I approached Dad about adopting the kids that lived with us, he would remind us that our duty was to help find their biological family for them and to pray for and support their relatives by encouraging bio families' relationships with the kids who lived with us. He always repeated to us that poverty is not a crime and that people make mistakes and get better. Then, he would remind us that our family strengths lay in the initial work with kids being taken by DCF and helping them recover. According to Dad, if we adopted, the beds and car would be full, and we would not carry that work on. So, that day, when he suddenly seemed to change his tune, we ignored his comment.

However, during the next three Bible studies he led, he said the same thing again—he felt in his heart that we should adopt. We still persisted in ignoring this though, since he had thoroughly convinced us that adoption was not what our family had been called to do. Plus, we did not even have any foster kids living with us at the moment.

A week later, Mom and I were doing homework when Dad called, asking for help logging into a site called "The Heart Gallery." It was then that Mom shifted. She looked at me after hanging up and said for the first time, "I think he's serious." So, we started praying about it and began looking at videos and pictures of kids who were available for adoption.

When my family shared a little bit with others about what we were doing, my parents started getting calls from people who had stories about adopted kids who were struggling and whose families were suffering. With all the information and warnings we were receiving,

Mom and Dad called a family meeting to talk about our feelings about potentially adopting. It was a pretty straightforward conversation to start. My sister and I both wanted to do it.

Mom nodded but clearly wanted us to go into this with our eyes wide open. "The well-meaning people who keep sharing these crazy adoption stories are absolutely right. We should expect difficulty along the way, although we won't know exactly in what form it will come ahead of time—only when we go through it."

She explained when a child who has been through so much hardship tries to integrate into a family, it prompts emotions and behaviors they do not always know how to handle—and the same goes for us. It can also be awkward and scary, and if we put ourselves into the shoes of a child going through an adoption, we would also have a set of struggles and react in complicated ways.

Mom also explained that not one of us in the room was any more special than a child who was waiting for a family, and they needed support and encouragement on their hard days and good days just like we do. "We may adopt a big sibling group, and some may do well, and some may go to jail or take drugs one day," my mom began. "Then, we love them, advocate for them, and pray for them in jail or at rehab or college or wherever they are. Hopefully, they do well, but we will not have outcome expectations when we adopt. The goal is to love the kids unconditionally where they are at, give out of our own abundance so that the children can flourish, and not expect any returns on that. If we keep our eyes on our mission statement, we will be fine no matter what happens." After a brief pause so her words could sink in, Mom continued. "We also will not force ourselves on anyone. There are kids and teens who prefer to stay in their foster or group homes, and we will honor that. We will be truthful and transparent about who we are and where our struggles are and what we can and cannot offer to adopted kids. Then, we will have done what we can to prepare, and we will not be overwhelmed, regardless of how things look on the surface."

After all this, my dad was the first to speak, breaking the serious tone that had set in. "JAIL?!" he said loudly with big eyes betraying the slightest twinkle in them. "Is my future kid going to run a jail ministry someday from the inside? Hopefully, we can help some kids avoid that. Only time will tell, so let's do this."

My dad came home with bios and videos of sibling groups with five and six kids in them. At that point, he and Mom would have heated discussions. We applied to be considered to adopt several of these groups of kids to see if we would be a good fit for anyone. Most of these groups of siblings had already been placed with an adoptive family, and no one had updated the adoption website. Some of the kids were several years older than the video showed, and a lot of times, the kids were not allowed to come to us because of my sister and me. "No other children in the home" was a quite common phrase attached to the kids' bios.

"What about this teen?" my mom asked my dad one night. "She is close to us, seems interested in education and sports like we are, and is about to age out of the system."

"Yes," Dad said. "Let's turn in an application on this group of five kids in Texas as well. We will keep the doors open and see what happens."

I was nervous about a large group of kids joining our family, and when we got a call from DCF that we had been chosen for a child, I held my breath. We clicked the link and saw it was the girl about to turn sixteen years old who lived only a couple of hours from us. We learned she had been in foster care for her entire life and had been waiting on a family to adopt her for almost as long. For her, time was quickly running out.

CHAPTER FIFTEEN

AN OLDER SISTER, I thought. I wondered what that would be like and imagined us playing sports together and hanging out. I was excited and hopeful for many reasons, one of them being one new sibling seemed less daunting than a large group all at once.

Since COVID was still going on, we got to know each other through Zoom. Latoya appeared on video sitting cross-legged on her bed in her room, her hair in a bonnet and her deep brown eyes framed by small glasses. She was beautiful. She was also talkative and smiled a lot, but I could tell she was struggling. Mom said she was having a lot of difficulty in school even though her testing showed she could understand the concepts. She had been moved to different foster homes due to challenges getting along with her foster families and some adoption placements that had not worked out. Latoya had guardian ad litems and other advocates working to help her move toward matching what she said her goals were with her actions. *Who doesn't go through that?,* I thought. I, too, struggled with the gap between what I said I wanted and knowing how to get there in my own life, so I felt I understood in some way what was happening. Latoya was doing much better than I would have in a similar situation, and I admired her happy spirit and willingness to connect with us.

Mom and Dad talked to Annabelle and me and said they felt like we might have the stability and skills to help Latoya, and I agreed. I wanted her as a sister if she wanted us. Annabelle was excited too.

My parents explained that if I had lived through some of the events Latoya had, I would likely have similar feelings and behaviors to hers, so it would be important to show her grace every day. Of course, we had been fostering for many years and taken in teens before, so I understood that it would not all be smooth sailing, but that we could probably help Latoya achieve some of her goals that would be harder to reach in foster care.

We started spending our weekends traveling to Jacksonville, where she had been born and lived in a string of foster homes for a lot of her life. My parents planned fun activities to help us get to know each other and try to bond. We raced go-carts, played in arcades, and participated in fun escape rooms, solving challenges together. We also went out to dinner as a family and ate her favorite foods and even played board games in our hotel room. We listened to Latoya's favorite music in the car and talked about different holiday traditions she had enjoyed. I loved these experiences we had together and will always cherish them.

DCF began bringing Latoya to us sometimes too. They gave my parents guidelines to follow in order to help her be healthy and safe according to her needs and history. Eventually, they brought her belongings as well, and she moved in as my foster sister even though everyone knew the goal was for her to be part of our family permanently. Mom put a big "Welcome Home" sign above our door and painted her room the baby pink color Latoya had requested. She also artfully arranged the pink bedspread and room decor she had picked out. We were so excited to show it to her; she couldn't get here fast enough.

When Latoya finally arrived, she was happy and tired. We helped her bring her belongings up to her new room, and she took a long nap on her big queen bed while Mom made dinner. We started to settle in.

It wasn't long before I was back to riding in the back seat while Latoya was driven to all kinds of appointments—just like always happened when someone new moved in. We got her glasses that fit her with a new prescription, let her choose a new hairdo, and went to a hairdresser/barbershop combo.

The day my sister got her hair braided, I walked over to the barbershop section. It was a new world for me—lots of guys hanging out talking, playing chess and checkers, and getting all kinds of designs shaved in their heads. I never knew a haircut could last hours, but I thought it was great. The ladies' side even offered to put cornrows in my hair that I had been growing out since my head had been shaved. They insisted it would get my hair out of my face. When they finished with my new 'do, they gave me a durag as well.

My mom watched with wide eyes. She seemed a little out of her element but smiled and read a magazine while my new sister and I relaxed there. When we got home, after doing a double take, Dad commented that he liked my hairdo. However, he did caution me that if I chose to keep the braids in my hair for school, most likely, a few people would be judgmental—and for contradictory reasons. I asked him if he cared, and after a moment, he said he did not. I said I did not either, and it was decided.

Latoya helped me put my durag on at night, and I learned to care for my new 'do. I was glad my parents had prepared me for when Monday hit, as they were not wrong. In case there had been any doubt left, I knew for sure now I would never fit in anywhere. By now, I was fine with that though.

Latoya asked if she could get her teeth straightened, and a few weeks later, she and I got braces put on the same day at the orthodontist. I rode in the back seat of the car when we drove her to tutoring, counseling, and sports training (she wanted to play softball, so Mom said it was important for her to train on the side a bit before school started back up). It took up so much time, but it was cool to see her whole personality come out. I loved seeing Latoya's happiness when she started feeling good about herself. Although she was not excited about it, she even agreed to attend church with us, which meant a lot to my parents. Most importantly, Latoya had more hope and excitement for her future.

A team of DCF workers had video meetings with Latoya and my parents regularly for months after the move to ensure everyone felt the fit was good, the guidelines DCF had asked my parents to follow were being kept, and each party wanted to keep moving toward adoption. Shortly before we finalized her adoption—via Zoom, of course, due to Coronavirus—she asked to change her name. "I want to be called Juanita!" she announced. She was clearly nervous about asking, and I could tell Dad was surprised at the request and did not know how to respond. He smiled after a beat and said that was a great name. "Let's talk to Mom about it," he suggested.

Latoya had been calling my parents Mom and Dad since our second visit, and it was not odd at all. All the kids that came to us had naturally done that or some variation of it. My parents were a mom and dad; some kids simply had multiple moms and dads. They would have been fine either way, but that was just the way it went.

Mom and Dad talked that night without Latoya during their evening walk, and as usual, I tagged along, riding my bike slowly next to them so I did not miss anything. Mom said she thought because she was passed between so many Latino homes in foster care, her culture was somewhat Latino. "Have you noticed her favorite foods are rice, beans, and mostly traditional Mexican dishes?" my mom asked. "She listens to Latino music exclusively, and the friends she had at her old school were Latino."

Dad said he wanted to support Latoya and was already trying hard to figure out how to best do that since this was an interracial adoption. Mom and Dad had already connected with our black friends and asked for help. My parents had explained from the beginning that if we ended up adopting outside our own race, we would probably be accused of trying to be "white saviors." But they loved Latoya. They knew she would not get adopted if they did not do it and decided they would not choose based on outsiders' criticism. Now, there was a new challenge: Latoya identified with Latino culture. How were we supposed to effectively support her?

In the end, they decided to support her choice while continuing to gently connect her to predominantly African American churches, concerts, restaurants, farmers' markets, friends, and a counselor who was black as well. Latoya offered to let my parents choose her middle name, and they selected "Kendi," the African name for "loved one." And so it would go, my dad being white; my mom, Latina; and my sister, black with a strong love for Hispanic culture. Then, there was me, somewhere in the middle of this, learning and soaking it all up.

They were right—people did judge us. And although they did not criticize me directly, I felt protective of my parents and our mission and goals, so it hurt me the same. People stared at us; criticized my parents for not focusing solely on Annabelle and me; accused them of adopting for the wrong reasons; said my parents' marriage would not survive it; accused them of preferential treatment of Juanita, Annabelle, or me, depending on the day—and on it went.

Since my parents had known this would be coming, we were often able to insulate ourselves. My family was very connected to other adoptive families who knew what we would go through and what we would need. We would spend time together, and when my parents shared their struggles, they received encouragement, support, comic relief, and a reminder to focus on the bigger picture despite some of the noise around us.

My school had accepted my new sister as a student, and they were incredibly supportive of her, helping her get her grades up so she could graduate and offering tutoring. They invited her onto the softball team and didn't question it when Latoya asked to be called Juanita moving forward. Our school even assisted her in getting college scholarships.

I watched from the sidelines and sometimes found myself completely intertwined with this redemptive work, as over the next two years, my parents and I, as well as our community, came alongside Juanita. We shared our name, our life, our resources as well as many meaningful days and many taxing ones with her.

Some of my favorite times were the trips we got to take together. We went on Christmas, Thanksgiving, and summer vacations and saw the blue water of the ocean as we floated lazily on rafts in the gulf and jumped over the big waves in the Atlantic. We watched colorful leaves fall from trees in the fall and played in snowstorms, built snowmen, and had snowball fights in the winter. I was overjoyed to experience all this alongside my big sister.

When Juanita turned seventeen, my dad knew it was time to teach her to drive. I was in the back of Mom's truck for these rides, Dad having decided not to teach another teen to drive in his truck for now. The whole experience felt similar to when Dad had taught Ava. Juanita was so excited, and my dad was visibly nervous. I was the fly on the wall that everyone seemed to have forgotten was there.

No one needed to tell me to buckle up as Juanita prepared to start the engine. Her hands were shaking as she gripped the steering wheel, but she was determined to learn. Dad gave her instructions on how to start the car and put it in gear. She pressed down on the gas pedal, and the car jolted forward, but Juanita quickly adjusted and kept it steady.

"Easy on the gas," Dad advised. "You don't want to give us whiplash."

Juanita let out a nervous giggle and followed his instructions as we drove around the neighborhood. I could not help but feel proud of her determination and bravery. It was not easy for anyone to learn how to drive, let alone someone who had gone through so much.

Dad had to correct Juanita many times, warning of mailboxes, curbs, and the occasional pedestrian. In the case of the latter, I held my breath as we passed. Dad's face turned red several times, and he frequently whisper-yelled and groaned and pumped imaginary brakes on his side of the car, his eyes as big as saucers. The whole experience to me was hilarious, scary, and inspiring all at once.

As we made our way back home at the end of that first lesson, Juanita's confidence grew, and she even started asking questions about the rules of the road. My dad patiently answered each of them, encouraging her all the way despite the clear rattling of his nerves.

When we pulled into the driveway, Juanita had a huge smile on her face. "I did it!" she exclaimed.

"You sure did." Dad beamed with pride.

The next day, we went out of the neighborhood for the first time with Juanita driving. Once again, Mom had declined to join us. Dad was riding shotgun, and I was in the back seat. We made it halfway up the main road before Dad lurched toward the driver's seat and jerked the steering wheel over. Juanita was drifting into the other lane and was about to veer into another car. I shrieked, and Dad loudly told me to be quiet. I decided this was not the time to proclaim my innocence, although I felt the warning yell had been appropriately timed.

We made it to the store, bought ice cream, and started to drive home. Dad promised not to say anything to stress us out on the trip back, and he almost stuck by his word.

We were almost home when we went around a curve that turned onto our street, and Juanita cut it close. I could see the tires might hit unless she made a correction fast. Dad's lips were white, his face was red, and the veins were popping out of his head as he finally gave up on his promise of sitting quietly and giving her a chance to drive without interference. He reached over quickly and tried to grab the wheel again. I could hear the scraping of metal on the curb as he reached out and jerked the wheel back. The beautiful truck rims that he regularly scrubbed clean for Mom by hand had just been scrubbed by concrete.

Dad told Juanita to pull off the road and stop the truck. Once she complied, he got out into the grass and stood wide-eyed for a moment, staring at the vehicle and then the ground. Juanita stepped out after a minute and said something to Dad. In response, he reached out for her, gave her a hug, and patted her head. When they came back to the truck though, Dad got behind the wheel to finish the drive home. His stress level had peaked, and the driving lesson was over.

I asked Dad if he could teach me to drive if Juanita was done for the day, and he shot me a look in the rearview mirror that suggested my timing may have been off. Eventually, he would give in though, and I learned to drive younger than all my siblings.

Dad kept taking Juanita out to drive even after that, and eventually, she was self-assured and in control. Even Mom rode shotgun and let Juanita chauffeur us around. I could see that this small victory meant so much more to Juanita than just learning how to drive. It was another sign that she was moving forward in life and overcoming her past. After getting comfortable behind the wheel, Juanita would take every opportunity to drive—whether it was running errands with my mom or taking Annabelle and me out for ice cream. And with each time behind the wheel, her confidence grew even more.

As I sat in the back seat during these drives, I could not help but feel grateful for having a big sister like Juanita. She may have come into our lives unexpectedly, but she had become such an important part of our family. I knew that no matter what challenges came our way, we would face them together—with Juanita behind the wheel and me along for the ride.

Two years went by quickly. I had turned twelve and then thirteen, and the time was approaching for me to finish seventh grade and for Juanita to graduate high school. Juanita wanted the full college experience, and when my parents could not convince her to stay home one more year to enjoy family life without the adult responsibilities and pressure, Mom went to work once again for her. She applied to every college in Florida on Juanita's behalf, encouraging them to offer her an opportunity at their school, reaching out to academic advisors all over the state with explanations for the dramatic grade shift in high school and why the school would be fortunate to have her. It was a busy season with much anticipation.

We also knew at this point that I would be skipping eighth grade and starting a dual enrollment college program for high school, so I was extremely interested in all the talks about higher education. I was always so excited when we did college visits or even watched videos of various universities and was secretly imagining myself in college. I loved to hear about the programs and clubs the schools had. I thought about my own future often during that season as my parents and sister prepared for her to go to college.

I was on a walk with my parents when Dad said to Mom, "You know, Michelle, there's a chance Juanita might not speak to us again once she heads to college. Based on her unique way of attaching to people, we shouldn't be surprised if that happens."

"I know," Mom acknowledged. "I've been wondering that in the back of my mind too. I am hopeful our relationship will improve once she has some more autonomy—I have heard of that happening too. Only time will tell."

"Hope so," Dad replied gruffly. "At the end of the day, it doesn't make any difference. We shared out of the abundance we had and not with expectations of getting something in return. The results are up to God. We just keep moving forward and try our best. If Juanita moves out and does not want to be in a genuine relationship with us, how does that change any of the measures of success over the last two years or the fun memories we made together or the positive impact her passing through our home has had on her and on us in so many ways? Since she couldn't stay with her biological family, I'm glad we've gotten to do life together with Juanita."

Mom nodded, and we walked quietly for a while. I asked the question that I guessed may have been on their minds as well. "Will we bring more kids into our home now?"

Mom and Dad glanced at each other and at me but did not respond. Ten years of this seemed to have made them tired, but I did not see our mission as having changed. However, Mom eventually responded with a question that I did not expect. "Do you think you will be involved in foster care or adoption when you're an adult, Ben?"

I looked at the horizon for a while and then at Mom. I thought about the blood, sweat, and tears that had come from this mission. I thought about all the time I did not get with my parents because they were helping another child, all the things I owned that had been broken or stolen, all the resources that had been used up and were now gone, some never to return. I thought about how misunderstood we had been at times.

I imagined what my life would have been like if we had not done it. My parents would not have repeatedly put me in the third row of the van so they could comfort a young stranger sitting closer to them. I would have had hundreds more hours to game, watch TV, play youth sports, hang with friends, and go where I wanted, do what I wanted, had I not been dragged around to hundreds of medical and educational appointments for someone else over the years.

I remembered when we were getting licensed and my parents had told me being a foster brother would hurt. There was no doubt—that had been the truth. I had the scars to prove it. But that was just a sliver of what my heart had felt throughout this whole experience.

Although I am not sure my parents expected a response, I shared with them what was swirling in my head. "I never thought about not being involved in helping children from hard places—that's what we do. I cannot imagine my life without all the brothers and sisters I have had, and I could not imagine something more important than that to spend my life on. I am grateful for the ways fostering and adopting opened my eyes and changed me, and I think I will always be involved. If I ever have biological kids, it would be good for them to be involved too."

Mom and Dad looked at me for a long time, as they often did, like I had caught them off guard. Dad's eyes were big as he met Mom's glance, and then he nodded slowly at me after a long pause. "Thank you for sharing that. I see you lean into the hard spaces instead of running from them. Your life has already been an impactful one already. I can also see how this journey has transformed each one of us for the better. Hopefully, one day, we will be out of a job, and kids will not need us anymore, but until then, I am glad you are in."

We finished our walk as the sun was setting and headed back up our driveway. "One day at a time," Dad said.

One day at a time, I thought. One yes at a time to a child that could have been me. One choice at a time to keep trying. One decision at a time to ignore criticism and judgment from those who would never truly walk a mile in our shoes. One step at a time beyond blood to family we haven't met yet. One life at a time changed—and mine most of all.

Q AND A WITH MICHELLE AND BEN

Q: What is the best part of fostering?

A: Michelle—Watching the kids' growth. We get to experience lots of fun firsts with the kids. Helping them learn to ride bikes, read, and drive; see the ocean for the first time; play sports or dance; jump on a trampoline; and eat fresh fruit. Things we take for granted are incredibly special to many kids we have done life with.

A: Ben—Getting to experience different cultures, traditions, and backgrounds and learn about different ways of life. I enjoyed growing together with the other kids, and they taught me so much. The love we had for each other during our time together is something that will always stay with me.

Q: How do you know when it is the right time to foster/adopt?

A: Michelle—I do not believe there is a "right time." The week we started the adoption process, my father-in-law was diagnosed with terminal cancer and given only a few months left to live. We had to decide whether to proceed, and after soul searching, we moved forward, walking alongside him during the dying process while adopting a child into our home. My father-in-law's funeral was held the day after our first adoption was finalized. We had an adoption party in the morning with all our family gathered in Georgia, and in the afternoon, we conducted my father-in-law's funeral. That is real life.

Q: Ben, was it hard for you to share your personal struggles in a public format? Why did you decide to do it?

A: Ben—It is hard to share struggles, but honestly, our lives have been somewhat public for a long time. The state must ask very personal questions and check on us to make sure the kids that live with us are safe, and after our first adoption, a lot of people watched our family and asked to share information about us. I like to study Bible characters, and I read about Paul, who did not hide his life even when he was in jail. I have not gone through anything like Paul did, but I am inspired by his story and want to live authentically as well, even in difficult times.

Q: What was the goal of this book for each of you?

A: Michelle—I have always said we are proof that anyone can be a foster family. Hopefully, this book helps families to be less scared to step out of their comfort zones, to see the value of being willing to struggle at times, and to think more about getting involved in sacrificial opportunities to change lives.

A: Ben—My goal was to give a perspective from a biological kid in a foster family. So many adults say they could not do it, as they want to protect the kids they already have, but I submit that keeping your kids away from hardship, sacrifice, and risk may not always be the best for them. It changed me for the better; it gave me a reality check, a sense of gratitude, and allowed me to practice focusing on others over myself.

Q: Michelle, did your marriage improve due to fostering? That seems unrealistic.

A: Michelle—Yes, and my relationship with my biological kids did too. You learn to be intentional and not to take the time you have with your loved ones for granted. It also forced us to stop focusing on ourselves so much, something we didn't even realize we were doing, and focus on a common goal to help others instead. It would be better, of course, if some day foster parents were not needed, but as it is now, there are benefits for the foster families themselves—not just the foster children.

Q: What has been the hardest part of fostering for each of you?

A: Michelle—Saying goodbye to kids that we care deeply for when sending them into situations we are unsure about. We do not make those decisions, of course, so we process and live through what others decide is best for the kids. We know the grieving process well and have learned with time to move through it as gracefully as possible.

A: Ben—Letting go. It's still hard to talk about. It's only hard to let go though because I miss so many of the kids that we did life with. Dealing with this is totally worth it. I understand that quote, "It's better to have loved and lost than never to have loved at all."

Q: Does your family really have a book with the names and pictures of every kid who has stayed with you?

A: Michelle—Absolutely. When we have a child who lived with us reach out, which happens often, I like to be able to show them they are important and special. So, I stay prepared with at least a few pictures and memories of each child. We want to be a backup or extended family for them when they seek us out.

Q: If your goal is to be family, then how can you send a child away? You wrote about moving a hard kid out.

A: Michelle—It has happened more than once, and it is heartbreaking. Safety concerns have forced the decision when we have had youth with unsafe behaviors. If we do not know with some confidence that we have the ability to keep the youth safe toward themselves and/or safe toward other children in the home, a move is the ethical choice.

Q: Aren't you mad at the biological parents when you see the shape the kids are in?

A: Michelle—There are definitely mixed feelings. I feel great empathy toward the adults who are struggling themselves, and I know that most of the time, they have had extremely difficult childhoods and often were in foster care themselves. But yes, in extreme cases, I struggle with anger and understanding things like choosing a romantic partner over a child (something that happens often).

Q: Is DCF as terrible as we hear?

A: Michelle—The humans that work in the DCF system are amazing, resilient, heartwarming, overworked, exhausted people. They are trying to prop up a system that works better in theory. Our experiences with employees in the system provided us with friendships and left us feeling cared for. But the system itself struggles to meet the needs of the children and carers at times. The issues are complicated, and those involved are working to improve it all the time.

Q: What are your goals for every foster child?

A: Michelle—Well, after the scare we had, we want them all to leave as proficient swimmers. We also want to partner with their bio families when possible and form long-term relationships with them. We hope every child leaves feeling they experienced love and support during a difficult time.

Q: Why did your bio kids go to different schools than your foster kids?

A: Michelle—Ben Jr. has different educational needs, as we discussed in the book, so he has moved schools a few times to accommodate his learning style. Ben's younger sister, Annabelle, is dyslexic and goes to a school that helps accommodate her needs. I tried from time to time to get some of our foster kids into these schools with our bio kids, but between the costs, the sudden arrivals and departures of the kids, and the fact that the schools generally run off a waitlist, it often did not work. When we were foster parents of a teen girl we eventually adopted, we were able to get her into the school with Ben Jr. The school was very supportive, and we were thankful.

Q: How do you all stay sane in the chaos?

A: Michelle—Time in nature, exercise, friends, hobbies, and leaning into my faith in God.

A: Ben—I have to cry sometimes, yell at the wall, and pray through it. I take time alone to process things. I also like to play chess and rollerblade and swim.

Q: What made you decide to adopt a teenager?

A: Michelle—It is a sad reality that teenagers are seen as less "adoptable." Attachment challenges, challenging behaviors, and the lack of ability for adoptive parents to influence early formative years are common fears people share that cause them to say no. Once we move past our fears, there is a big opportunity available to disrupt the normal flow of things for the positive, especially with teens who are in danger of aging out of the system. Expanding our view of what a successful teen adoption looks like may give people more freedom to step into these meaningful relationships and share out of their own abundance without as many expectations in return. When we went through our first adoption, our sixteen-year-old daughter received a new birth certificate and, for the first time, had a father to list on it. Things like that matter, even if you adopt a young adult who is preparing to age out of the system and live independently.

Q: What about all the attachment talk, gentle parenting, and connected parenting?

A: Michelle—Yes, these are excellent, important educational pieces for families involved in this work. We are always learning new skills and trying to put them into practice. Often, we do well. But we are humans, and we have parenting failures too. Some of these are mentioned in this book. As far as attachment goes, it does look different for various kids. Often, kids follow us around like a lost puppy. Other times, they will not let us anywhere near them. Many challenges with kids who have lived in foster care are related to attachment differences. Therefore, goals, closeness, and wins for each of your children, whether biological, foster, or adopted, will look different depending on how they are individually progressing.

Q: How do you keep everything fair with the different kids?

A: Michelle—We cannot handle everything the same way for each child that lives with us. We meet each child where they are and parent them individually according to their needs, not according to one of the other child's needs. So, it's true—two kids of the same age may have different privileges or a different structure in place from one another. However, one thing we are careful of is to try to spend the same amount of quality time with each child.

Q: You talk in the book about being judged. Is that really a problem? I think foster parents are saints.

A: Michelle—It is a problem, and my husband is great at reminding me to look away and keep going. Sometimes, our foster kids are creative storytellers when they are mad at us. Many excellent foster homes are falsely accused of abuse. We are fortunate that this never happened to us. There is a system in place to investigate and clear the names of families when they are falsely accused. At times, people insinuate that we are harming our bio kids, harming our marriage, or harming the kids we are trying to help. My husband reminds me the only way to prevent criticism is to do nothing.

Q: How did you write this book together?

A: Ben—We talked and brainstormed ideas together a lot initially and shared memories with each other. Then, I just talked (am I allowed to say word-vomited?) while Mom typed next to me. Occasionally, if it was too late at night and Mom was sleeping, I would use the audio-to-text feature and talk to Microsoft Word. I'd send Mom the document after, and she would incorporate it into what we had already done. It was an emotional process, and we laughed and cried together while writing it.